Bloody Women

Ireland's Female Killers

David M. Kiely

Gill & Macmillan

Gill & Macmillan Ltd
Goldenbridge
Dublin 8
with associated companies throughout the world
www.gillmacmillan.ie

© David M. Kiely 1999

0 7171 2852 0
Print origination by David's Digital Dynamics
Printed by Caledonian International
Book Manufacturing Ltd, Glasgow

A catalogue record is available for this book from
the British Library.

1 3 5 4 2

Bloody Women

Ireland's Female Killers

For McKenna

Contents

Mention the name Myra Hindley and a single image invariably springs to mind. That of a young woman with bleached-blonde hair, who fixes the onlooker with a withering stare from cold, black eyes, the mouth set in an ugly, defiant line. Never mind that the real Hindley, serving a life sentence in Broadmoor prison, looks not at all like the woman in this picture – the first image is the one we associate with murder most horrifying.

Hindley shocked us more than thirty years ago. We were shocked because she'd been found guilty of assisting Ian Brady in his torture and murder of children. We were also shocked because Hindley was a woman.

Women are not supposed to murder. This is, by tradition, a man's domain. Women are 'the gentler sex'. Women are expected to bring new life into the world, not take life from it.

So what drives a woman to break the Fifth Commandment? Research suggests that there's little difference – if any at all – between the sexes in matters of motivation. Pride, covetousness, lust, greed and anger rank highly among the deadly catalysts to murder, as the following pages show. It's also fair to say that, in some instances, the woman has been sinned against, and the victim turns the tables on her persecutor.

Certainly women kill less often than men. Since 1976, when the United States restituted the death penalty, of a total of 6,180 killers sentenced to execution 116 were women. In other words, scarcely more than 2% of American murderers are female.

Surprisingly enough, Irishwomen appear to be more

murderous than their American sisters. In 1995 the crim-
inologist Dr Enda Dooley published a study of serious
crime, *Homicide in Ireland 1972–1991*. He concluded
that during those two decades crime in the Republic of
Ireland had increased – but predominantly property
crime. There was also an increase in violent crime, yet
this 'has not been mirrored in an increase in the overall
homicide rate as stated in official statistics'. Dooley cites
587 killings and gives us a breakdown according to the
gender of the perpetrators: 545 were committed by men,
42 by women. This means that women committed 7.2%
of murders between 1972 and 1991 – more than three
times the US statistic.

Yet it's still a small proportion. So small that, when a
woman is arraigned for murder, her trial generates im-
mense public interest; some would say a disproportion-
ate amount. The public gallery of the law court fills with
spectators come to dwell on every word of the prosecution, as the details of the deadly deed emerge.

The 'how' of a killing perpetrated by a woman can be
of as much interest as the 'why'; we want to know what
weapon she used. The pages of *Bloody Women* show that
there's no real weapon of feminine choice. To be sure,
poison recurs – there are three instances of women using
strychnine. This is understandable: poison does not involve the use of force. Moreover until recent times a
woman could obtain poison more easily than a divorce or
legal separation. Nowadays women kill using a variety of
weapons, ranging from the blunt to the sharp, from the
silent to the explosive.

If you were ever in doubt, then the following pages will
convince you that, in certain species of life on earth, the
female can be deadlier than the male.

ACKNOWLEDGEMENTS

This book would have been impossible to prepare without the help and encouragement of a great many people. I wish to thank them all – and hope that those whose contributions I may have omitted will forgive the oversight.

Thanks first to Jonathan Williams, my literary agent and editor, for securing this and other commissions; to Fergal Tobin, my publisher, for entrusting me with the job; to Christina McKenna for shouldering a sizable chunk of the research; to Sean and Colette Sloan for securing the hardware; to Damian Hogan of the Garda Press Office; to Gregory O'Connor of the National Archives, Mark Wilson of the *Belfast Telegraph*, Kathleen Bell of the *Irish News* and Emma James of Forum Press for pointing my research in the right directions; to the ever-helpful and courteous librarians and staff of the National Library of Ireland; to the even more helpful and courteous librarians and staff of the Central Library, Belfast; to Nicholas Davies, whose work I greatly relied on in the telling of the Susan Christie case; to Tom Reddy, whose books on Irish murders were indispensable; to Joe Baker, editor of *Belfast Murders*, whose help with the Northern Ireland material was invaluable; to Linda Giles, who lent me her books and gave encouragement; and lastly no thanks whatsoever to the Open University, Milton Keynes and Belfast.

Kate Webster and her Heavy Black Bag

What is it about Victorian crime that seldom fails to send a thrill of terror down the spine? Perhaps it's because such crime took place at the start of the modern era, when forensic science as we know it was still in its infancy. When procedures we now take for granted were being carefully tested, gingerly tried. Think of fingerprinting, think of ballistic tests.

At the same time, the Victorians appear far removed from our own ways of thinking and doing. A different ethic seemed to apply; in many ways their world appears alien and macabre.

Or could it be that fictional accounts of Victorian sleuthing have the upper hand in our psyche? Is Sherlock Holmes not the Victorian detective par excellence?

So much for the heroes. Think of the villains. We read with horror about Jack the Ripper and wonder how such a monster could have remained at large, defying all attempts to bring him to justice. Our image of Victorian England is coloured by the many versions of the Ripper story. We see the London fog, the mist on the Thames, the mean cobbled streets and alleyways of Whitechapel with their prostitutes on every corner. It all seems so real to us, thanks to film and television.

But is it real? Did such monsters exist? Unfortunately, yes, they did. One of them was female – and Irish to boot.

Kate Webster, née Lawler, was born in Enniscorthy, County Wexford, in 1849. She would claim to have been married at one time to a sea captain named Thomas Webster, by whom she had four children, though none survived to adolescence. Her life of crime appears to have begun early; at the age of fourteen she was arrested and imprisoned in Dublin for petty theft. On her release she settled in Liverpool sometime in the 1860s and turned to petty crime – larceny and the like. She was arrested several times and got to know the inside of many jails before moving to London in 1873.

We have only her word to go on that she intended at this point to mend her ways and try to lead an honest life. What is known is that she lived for a time with a man named Strong and gave birth to a fifth child, a boy she doted on. He was five when Kate knocked on the door of Julia Thomas, a widow, on 27 January 1879.

Mrs Thomas had lived at various addresses since the death of her second husband in 1873. The last was 2 Mayfield Cottages, Richmond, close to where the Thames winds lazily past Kew Gardens. At the time, that vast conurbation called Greater London did not yet exist; Richmond, like its neighbours Brentford, Barnes, Norwood and Chiswick, were pleasant little villages far from the city smoke.

Mrs Thomas lived alone and employed a servant to take care of the household duties. None stayed long. By all accounts the widow was an eccentric, though not in the genial sense. She bullied and tormented those unlucky enough to work for her and they came and went more often than the widow changed addresses. Mayfield Cottages was her sixteenth home since the death of her husband.

Mrs Thomas had airs. She lived on a small income yet liked to give the impression of being wealthy. Her clothes and jewellery were extravagant and the sight of the widow strolling in Richmond Park, laden with baubles and clad in finery to rival that of a duchess, never failed to excite comment in the locality.

She cannot, however, have been particularly bright (or discerning) because when she interviewed her latest 'victim', Kate Webster, she made no inquiries into the Irishwoman's background. Had she done so, then many unsavoury facts might have emerged – not least being the fact that Kate had but recently been released from prison where she'd served twelve months for theft. As it was, Mrs Thomas asked for no references but offered Kate a job solely on the commendation of a friend, who cannot have known Kate all that well. Had this been the case then the friend would have been acquainted with Kate's history of petty crime. She was also dangerous, had a dreadful temper, and had once beaten an employer senseless.

The relationship between mistress and servant was doomed from the start. Mrs Thomas was fussy and overbearing; nothing a servant did could satisfy her. Kate was resentful and vindictive. At first she suffered the black moods and temper of her employer in silence, but before long the little two-storey house became too confining for such strong-willed women. Kate rebelled; Mrs Thomas returned the insults in kind. Kate counter-attacked with yet more defiance and outright venom.

Mrs Thomas began to grow concerned. What, she

wondered, have I let into my home? She gave Kate notice to quit at the end of February 1879. The situation had become so serious that Mrs Thomas was genuinely afraid of her servant. She never risked being alone with Kate and invited some friends from the local church to stay with her: a mother and daughter. Unfortunately the guests' departure did not coincide with Kate's; they left on 28 February; Kate drew in her horns and persuaded her employer to allow her to remain until Monday, 3 March.

On Tuesday, shortly before seven o'clock, a coalman named Henry Wheatley stopped his horse and cart near Barnes Bridge, about a mile from Park Road, Richmond. He'd caught sight of a wooden box lying partially submerged in the water near the bank of the Thames.

Wheatley thought he might have stumbled on something of value and told his mate he wanted to investigate. He went down and dragged the box out of the water. It was made of deal and had a hinged lid. He cut the twine that secured it. The lid fell back, revealing the contents.

Wheatley, a man of stout constitution, was revolted. Instead of the hoped-for treasure he saw a mass of flesh that had a light, almost white, appearance. He called his mate over; the mate shrugged off the find as being no more than a selection of cuts from a butcher's shop that had found their way, either by accident or design, into the river. Wheatley thought otherwise: he thought he recognized human body parts among the flesh.

He hurried to Barnes police station to report his discovery; three constables returned with him to the spot, accompanied by Dr James Adams, a police surgeon.

As Wheatley watched in ghastly fascination, Adams carefully drew the mass of twisted, mutilated flesh from the deal box and laid it, piece by piece, on the ground.

The pieces formed the body of a woman. The corpse was almost intact, save for a foot and three fingers – and the head.

Adams thought he could account for the pallor of the flesh. It displayed moreover little trace of decomposition. His verdict: somebody had *boiled* the remains.

Mrs Josie Hayhoe owned the Hole in the Wall inn on Park Road, Richmond. At about nine o'clock on Monday evening a female customer had entered. Mrs Hayhoe knew her; Kate Webster was in the habit of enjoying a gin and tonic there at weekends or on her day off.

This particular night, though, Kate wasn't buying; she was selling. She reached into her bag, took out two jars filled with a greasy, milk-white substance, and placed them on the counter. They contained, Kate declared, 'the best dripping'.

Mrs Hayhoe declined the offer. Whether Kate had more success elsewhere when peddling her cooking fat, we do not know.

The following day – the same day as Wheatley's grisly find – the Porters, a family living in Hammersmith, received a visitor they'd known in 1873 but who'd lost touch with them. Kate – they never knew her surname – had lived next door to them. She'd given them to understand she was a maidservant, then temporarily unemployed.

The new Kate Webster was not as the Porters remembered her. Gone were the cheap clothes and fake jewellery. She had every appearance of a well-to-do London lady.

'Kate!' a surprised Henry Porter said. 'I should never have recognized you if you'd not spoken first.'

The woman who presented herself at their door was dressed in a beautifully tailored jacket and a silk gown that exuded expense. She wore two gold necklaces, gold earrings, a gold brooch and gold rings on her fingers.

She also carried with her a capacious black bag, not unlike those used by doctors. Its soberness seemed not in keeping with her outfit.

Kate had much to tell the Porters. She'd married a certain Mr Thomas, she said, a man of some wealth. Alas, her husband had died recently and she wished to return to Ireland. She wanted to sell her property: a house at Mayfield Cottages, Richmond, bequeathed to her by an aunt. She'd no wish to live in that house any longer, she told them sadly; it held painful memories for her. Would Mr Porter be so kind as to arrange for the house and furniture to be sold? Mr Porter very gallantly agreed; he knew a broker who'd take care of everything.

They discussed the matter further over afternoon tea. Mr Porter promised to visit the house and inspect its contents. Kate was delighted. There was, she said, another little matter that Porter's son Robert might be able to help her with. She didn't specify what it was; she called it simply 'a task'. Again Mr Porter assured the widowed 'Mrs Thomas' of his assistance, and it was decided that Robert should accompany Kate back to Richmond.

Throughout the meal the big black bag rested under the table at her feet.

They didn't hail a cab to bring Kate back to Hammersmith train station. It was a fine spring afternoon and Mr Porter offered to accompany her the relatively short distance there. And so they set off: Kate, Porter and Porter junior. Fifteen-year-old Robert shared his father's gallantry and on seeing that the black bag was growing too heavy for 'Mrs Thomas', volunteered to carry it for her.

It proved far heavier than the boy had expected, and he wondered about its contents. Soon the bag grew too heavy for the boy as well and he asked his father to relieve him of the burden. Henry Porter too was surprised by the weight – he calculated it to be between twenty and twenty-five pounds.

There was a public house quite close to Hammersmith Bridge: the Oxford and Cambridge Arms. Kate suggested they rest there for a while; she wished to treat Mr Porter and his son to some refreshment for their pains. There was also another matter. She must bring the black bag to a friend who lived nearby in Barnes. Would they mind waiting?

She returned twenty minutes later. Without the bag.

The trio arrived at Hammersmith station at about nine o'clock; Mr Porter bade goodbye to Kate and young Robert. During the short train journey she told the boy what the 'task' entailed. There was a box that had to be delivered to another friend, one who lived on the other side of Richmond Bridge. It wasn't that heavy, Kate said; simply awkward for one person to carry alone. With Robert's help it would prove no trouble at all.

Seated in Kate's living-room the boy must surely have asked himself why the widow could not have had a cab-driver help her with the box. Money, after all, would have been no obstacle for the clearly wealthy Mrs Thomas. . . . No, no, she told him; you need only help me halfway across the bridge; I've arranged to meet my friend there. She poured Robert a glass of rum; it was close to eleven.

In the event the box turned out to be heavier and more awkward to carry than Robert had been led to believe. The rough twine that held shut its lid chafed his hands as he helped the 'widow' lug it down the street and across Richmond Bridge.

They rested at the spot appointed for the rendezvous: an iron seat in the recess to one side of the central arch. Night had fallen by this time; the dark Thames flowed beneath them.

Kate suggested it was senseless for both to wait there in the cold.

'Put it down and you go on back,' she said. 'My friend will be here directly. I'll catch you up.'

Robert headed back the way they'd come. No sooner had he reached the middle of the bridge than he heard a splash from below. He looked over the parapet but saw nothing in the blackness. Kate reappeared. Her friend, she told him, had taken charge of the box. All was well.

Robert's father, good as his word, had managed to find a broker for Kate's furniture. John Church was the proprietor of the Rising Sun pub in Hammersmith. He came to the house the following week, cast his eye over the furniture and agreed to take it off her hands. Kate haggled over the price – and would continue to haggle for days. In all the publican paid eight visits to 2 Mayfield Cottages. Eventually a price was agreed and arrangements were made for him to call on 18 March.

Kate grew friendly with Church during that second week in March. They shared a glass or two in a local tavern; she introduced her son to him and spoke warmly of her fictitious husband, the late Mr Thomas. Church put her in touch with Henry Weston, a Hammersmith greengrocer who owned a van that might be suitable for removing the furniture.

On the appointed day, the murdered woman's house

was a hive of activity. Weston the grocer came with two vans. Church showed up, as did Henry Porter. The removal was bound to attract attention in Mayfield Cottages – and it did. As Church and his helper were busy loading the vans the door of the house next door opened and Miss Elizabeth Ives, the occupant, appeared. She was puzzled.

'I should like to know where the furniture is going,' she demanded of Kate.

'Mrs Thomas has sold it' was the reply. Miss Ives looked doubtful and Kate followed this up with: 'The man can show you the receipts. Mr Weston is going to take it to Hammersmith.'

Then Miss Ives, not unnaturally, enquired about her next-door neighbour. 'I haven't seen Mrs Thomas for about a fortnight now,' she said. 'Do you know where she is?'

Kate was all too aware of the widow's whereabouts. She also knew her cover was about to be blown. John Church had come within earshot; he'd been engaged by a 'Mrs Thomas'. He looked at her queerly.

'I don't know,' Kate replied to Miss Ives's query. 'I don't know.'

What Kate also didn't know was that Mrs Thomas had rented the house – and a good deal of the furniture – from Miss Ives. No wonder the lady was asking awkward questions. Church sensed that something was up and decided to return the furniture to the house. Miss Ives went in search of her estate agent. Kate went back into the house and grabbed a bundle of dresses. She left with Henry Porter and they made their way to Church's pub, the Rising Sun, where Kate left the dresses in the safe-keeping of Mrs Church.

Next on the itinerary was the Porter home where Kate had left her son. He was asleep when they arrived but she demanded he dress at once. She'd a cab waiting. Kate explained that she was bringing the boy to her father.

This was her second mistake that day. The first was leaving the dresses in Mrs Church's care.

Meanwhile the finding of the box and its ghastly contents had been reported at length in the London papers. Henry Porter had read about it and his son Robert had told him of the errand 'Mrs Thomas' had asked him to run. Father and son compared notes; the box found in the Thames matched the description Robert gave.

Then Mrs Church began going through the dresses left with her. She found papers: letters addressed to the real Mrs Thomas and some other personal items. She told her husband and he told Henry Porter.

The two men paid a visit to somebody who'd written to Mrs Thomas, a Mr Menhennick of Finsbury Park. The man hadn't heard from Mrs Thomas in some time. Nor did his description of the lady remotely fit that of Kate Webster. Kate was well built, had fair hair and freckles. And the real Mrs Thomas certainly didn't speak with a pronounced Irish accent. Menhennick went to his solicitor; the solicitor, joined by Church and Porter, alerted the police in Richmond.

Next day the three men went to 2 Mayfield Cottages in the company of Inspector John Pearman, and made a thorough search. There were traces of blood in various parts of the kitchen; stains so stubborn that they hadn't yielded to scrubbing. The men found pieces of burnt clothing and charred bones among the embers of the kitchen fire. Pearman discovered a razor in the scullery and a chopper hidden in a cupboard. Both were tested later for bloodstains and the tests proved positive. The inspector also found the handle of a box which fitted the one fished out of the Thames. He was convinced he knew where Mrs Thomas had met her end.

For somebody who'd taken such care to dispose of a corpse and cover her tracks, Kate Webster as good as led the authorities right to her door. She'd told Henry Porter she was bringing her son to Ireland, to her father. Inspector Pearman found one of Kate's dresses in the house and in a pocket was a letter giving her uncle's address. Pearman telegraphed his Irish colleagues. They visited the house – in the village of Killane, birthplace of John Kelly, the giant revolutionary, commemorated in song. Ten days after her flight from England, Kate Webster was arrested. She was charged the following day and brought back to London. But not before she made a statement so barefaced that it beggars belief.

She accused John Church of complicity in the murder. She repeated this statement in Richmond Police Station and Church was duly arrested.

According to Kate, she'd known Church for many years, and they'd even been lovers. She tried to convince the police that he it was who'd devised the plan to murder Mrs Thomas so they could get their hands on her property. Next she attempted to implicate Henry Porter.

The presiding magistrate, however, was having none of it. Church had an excellent alibi for the night of the murder and other pertinent dates: he'd been serving pints of ale in his tavern and had any number of witnesses to prove it. Within the hour the magistrate had ordered the charges against both men dropped, and Kate was sent for trial at the Central Criminal Court.

The proceedings caused a sensation when they opened on 2 July 1879. The prosecution assembled a great number of witnesses whose testimony was damning. Not least among them was Mary Durden, a milliner, who'd known Kate for four years.

'I saw her on Shrove Tuesday, the twenty-fifth of February, at my house,' she said of the accused. 'She told me she was going to Birmingham to see about some property which her aunt had left her. She told me she had a letter from her aunt telling her where to find her gold watch and chain and her jewels, and everything her aunt had was to come to her.'

From this it was clear that Kate had planned the murder at least a week in advance. There was only one witness who gave evidence pertaining to the actual night of the killing: Miss Elizabeth Ives, the owner of the house. She had, she deposed, heard voices from next door, those of at least two men and a woman calling to somebody named 'Lizzie'. . . .

The expert witnesses described the finding of the box and its contents – much to the horror of the court and those in the public gallery. Inspector Pearman told of the bloodstains and charred bones in the kitchen, and the implements used to dismember the corpse.

Kate was found guilty.

Before pronouncing the inevitable sentence of death the judge asked her if she'd anything to say in her defence. She exonerated Church and Porter yet tried to pin the murder on a man not present: Strong, the father of her child. She also claimed to be pregnant again, in the hope that this 'fact' might mitigate in her favour.

Mr Justice Denham had heard enough lies. Donning the black cap, he fixed the date of the execution.

We shall never know what really happened in Richmond on the night of 2 March 1879. Before Kate Webster went to the scaffold, however, she made a long statement, some of which is given here. While much is obvious fabrication, it does describe in brutal and shocking detail how Kate disposed of the corpse of the woman she'd murdered.

Bear in mind that she made the statement on the eve of her execution and therefore had nothing to gain by lying about the means by which she'd achieved this.

> I entered the lady's service in the month of January. At first I thought her a nice old lady, and imagined that I could be comfortable and happy with her; but I found her very trying.
>
> She used to do many things to annoy me. When I had finished my work in the rooms she used to go over it and point out places where she said I did not clean, thus showing evidence of a nasty spirit towards me.
>
> This sort of conduct made me have an ill-feeling towards her, but I had no intention of killing her, at least not then.
>
> One day I had an altercation with her, and we mutually arranged I should leave her service, and she made an entrance to that effect in her memorandum book.
>
> On the Sunday evening, 2nd March last, Mrs Thomas and I were alone in the house. We had some argument at which she and myself were enraged, and she became very agitated and left the house to go to church in that state, leaving me at home.

Upon her return from church, before her usual hour, she came in and went upstairs. I went up after her. We had an argument which ripened into a quarrel, and in the height of my anger and rage I threw her from the top of the stairs to the ground floor. She had a heavy fall. I felt that she was seriously injured, and I became agitated at what had happened, lost control of myself, and, to prevent her screaming or getting me into trouble, I caught her by the throat and in the struggle she was choked.

I threw her on the floor. I then became entirely lost and without any control over myself, and looking on what had happened, and the fear of being discovered, I determined to do away with the body as best I could.

I chopped the head from the body with the assistance of a razor, which I used to cut through the flesh afterwards. I also used the meat-saw and the carving knife to cut the body up with. I prepared the copper [a boiler for laundry, etc.] with water to boil the body to prevent identity; and as soon as I had succeeded in cutting it up I placed it in the copper and boiled it. I opened the stomach with the carving knife, and burned up as much of the parts as I could.

During this time there was nobody in the house but myself. When I looked upon the scene before me and saw the blood around my feet, the horror and dread I felt was inconceivable.

I was bewildered, acted as if I was mad,

and did everything I possibly could to conceal the occurrence, keep it quiet and everything regular, fearing the neighbours might suspect something had happened. I was greatly overcome, both from the horrible sight before me and the smell, and I failed several times in my strength and determination, but was helped on by the devil in this vile purpose.

I remained in the house all night, endeavouring to clear up the place and clean away the traces of murder.

I burned one part of the body after chopping it up, and boiled the other. I think I boiled one of the feet. I emptied the copper, throwing the water away after having washed and cleaned the outside. I then put parts of the body into the little wooden box which was produced in Court, and tied it up with cord, and determined to deposit it in the Thames, which was afterwards done (in the manner already described) with the help of young Porter.

I remember the coalman, Mr Deane, coming to the house and knocking at the door. I was greatly frightened, but in dread of creating suspicion I opened the door to answer him, and spoke to him, as he stated in his evidence. When he called I was engaged in regulating the place, and was in a dreadful state of mind.

I also recall a young lady calling at the house about the repairs, and I answered her in the manner she gave in her evidence.

I put the head of Mrs Thomas in the black bag, and being weary and afraid to remain in the house, I carried it to the Porters, and had some tea there. I placed the bag with the head in it under the tea table, and afterwards took it away from the house and disposed of it in the way and in the place I have described to my solicitor, Mr O'Brien.

The deposition of this black bag gave me great uneasiness. I feared I might be discovered and the identity of Mrs Thomas thereby proven, and when I heard that a black bag had been found I was greatly troubled. I pretended to Mr O'Brien that the bag contained nothing of the kind. The foot found in the dung-hill at Kingston was placed there by me, for when I came to realize the true state of things and the great danger I stood in, I resolved to do all in my power to keep everything secret and prevent being discovered.

When I placed the box in the river and disposed of the head and other parts of the body as best I could, and cleared up the place so that a person coming in might not suspect or see anything irregular, it was suggested to my mind to sell all that there was in the house and go away; and with that view I went and saw Porter, and introduced the sale of the things to him.

He accompanied me to Church's, and we bargained for the sale in the manner set forth in the evidence given at the trial respecting that part of the transaction. I gave the chairs to Porter as a gift, and also kept on ordering things for the house from trades people in order to evade suspicion.

At the time of the murder I took possession of Mrs Thomas's gold watch and chain, and also of all the money in the house, which was only seven or eight pounds. I accompanied Church to the watchmaker's and asked for Mrs Thomas's watch. Church only paid me £13, not £18 as stated.

I did not murder Mrs Thomas from any premeditation. I was enraged and in a passion, and I cannot now recollect why I did it; something seemed to seize me at the time. I threw her downstairs in the heat of passion and strong impulse; I acted towards her as I have described. I never had a hatred or what may be termed a bad feeling towards anybody in my lifetime, certainly not such as would ever have induced me to do them bodily injury; and I cannot account for the awful feelings that came over me from the time Mrs Thomas came home from church until the murder was completed. . . .

I die with great fortitude and confidence in my faith, and in Blessed God, whom I beseech to have mercy on my soul.

Before closing, it might be interesting to speculate on the state of Kate Webster's mind prior to and at the time of the murder. It was a premeditated killing, certainly – as the milliner's testimony showed, and I have no doubt that Kate didn't shirk from it when the time came.

But was she in complete possession of her mental faculties at the time? She confessed she 'was helped on by the devil in this vile purpose', and probably truly believed this. When she made this statement it was too late to save her skin, and she knew it.

Yet one woman's demonic possession is another's schizophrenia – or even split personality. Kate's account of her behaviour reads oddly; it's as though she's describing the actions and emotions of two people. The one is aghast at her 'accidental' throttling of Mrs Thomas and revolted by the means by which she disposes of the body. The other thinks nothing of trying to sell the fat boiled from the corpse.

At least one portion of the statement is enigmatic, to say the least:

> There is no truth in the evidence given by Miss Ives that she heard men talking in the house on Monday night or the voice of a woman calling Lizzie. Miss Ives is mistaken in that part of the evidence, as there was nobody in the house but myself; and the statement I made that Strong and a woman were in the house is untrue. I made these statements to save myself, if possible, from my perilous position.

Elizabeth Ives was certain she'd heard more than one voice raised that night – when Mrs Thomas was already dead. Kate subsequently stated she was alone.

So why did Miss Ives hear someone calling the name 'Lizzie'?

Ann Porter, Henry's wife, testified before the magistrate's court that she'd known Kate six years before. Kate, she stated, had shared lodgings with a young woman known only to the Porters as Lizzie. She ran a laundry.

Who was calling for Lizzie that night in Mayfield Cottages? Was that person calling to Miss Ives – to Elizabeth Ives? It seems highly unlikely; Mrs Thomas wasn't on such familiar terms with the landlady; nor was Kate Webster.

Was Kate talking to some part of herself, a part calling itself Lizzie? Had she convinced herself that Lizzie, not herself, had murdered? Such delusion is not unknown.

Whatever the answer, Kate Webster took it with her to the gallows. She was executed at Wandsworth Prison on 29 July 1879. The black bag containing the severed head of Mrs Thomas was never found.

Jane Lawther and her Mother, the Child-Killers

It was that great nineteenth-century master of horror fiction, Edgar Allan Poe, who described best what most of us consider to be the ultimate nightmare: that of being buried alive.

That such an appalling fate can overcome one in real life is more than a possibility. There are many instances on record of coffins being exhumed, coffins whose lids bore traces of *nail-marks* on the inside – dreadful evidence of the unlucky occupant's futile struggle for freedom. It hardly bears thinking about.

Yet among the court records – and still etched on the folk memory of Belfast – is the shocking account of a woman who, aided by her husband and with the connivance of her mother, arranged to have her own newborn son buried – in full knowledge that the infant was still living.

The story begins in that district of east Belfast known as Ballymacarrett. It's a relatively poor area on the right bank of the river Lagan; in 1884 it was a collection of mean streets housing working-class folk.

On a dark Sunday evening in November a gravedigger called William Spence opened his door to an elderly widow. He knew her well. She was Jane McCracken, an acquaintance of his wife's family.

Mrs McCracken made of Spence an odd request. She wished to have her family plot opened in order that her daughter might bury a newly born baby. The boy had been born two months premature, she said – and had never breathed. Could it be done as speedily as possible? Say, early the next morning?

Spence hesitated. He suspected that all was not what it should be. He knew it was highly unusual for a bereaved person – or her mother for that matter – to approach a gravedigger direct; the normal procedure was to contact Spence's employers, the Belfast Board of Guardians, the body responsible for Knock Burial Ground, where Mrs McCracken's husband was interred.

The widow hastened to ease Spence's conscience: she offered him five shillings for his trouble, payable on completion of the job. Spence turned to his wife for guidance. Five shillings was a tidy sum. The gravedigger assured Mrs McCracken he'd take care of it first thing the next day. The widow told him her son-in-law would be along with a cart; he'd pick Spence up at his home.

While the deal was being struck in Ballymacarrett another was being made in the same vicinity, in a house in Ivanhoe Street. John Lawther, a twenty-six-year-old carpenter, was paying a call on William Fitzsimons, carter by trade. The carter was sleeping; he was an early riser. His father admitted Lawther and went to rouse his son.

Lawther had an errand for the carter; he wished to charter his vehicle. Could he, he asked, collect Lawther at his home at six the next morning? Fitzsimons agreed; though better make it half past six, he said, just to be on the safe side.

Fitzsimons set off the following day to keep his appointment at the address given: 55 Abbot Street, in the Ormeau Road area. He found Lawther waiting for him at the corner of Fitzsimons's own street. Evidently Lawther was in a hurry – or was determined that the carter would keep his side of the bargain. He climbed aboard and they travelled to Abbot Street.

Fitzsimons was invited in by Lawther's wife Jane. Would he, she asked, care for a drink? It was a little early in the day but Fitzsimons accepted a bottle of stout. 'For later,' he said. Then Jane Lawther explained the nature of the errand. There was a coffin – a small one – that must be brought to Knock Burial Ground for interment. It contained the remains of her infant son.

Fitzsimons smelled a rat. His cart was not a hearse, he protested, and for him to use it as one would be against the law.

'It's perfectly all right,' Jane assured him. 'My mother made arrangements with the gravedigger; he's waiting for you.' Everything was above board.

The carter gave in, though with some reluctance. He hoisted the coffin – it weighed almost nothing – onto his cart. Mr Lawther covered it with a sheet and the pair set off. They collected the gravedigger at his home, as arranged, and drove the short distance to the cemetery. It lay to the east of the city; in 1884 the sprawl of Belfast had not yet extended to the townland of Knockbreda. They arrived a little before eight o'clock.

There was a small wooden hut just inside the entrance. Spence the gravedigger called it 'my porter lodge'. There was a little table, two chairs and a stove – unlit at the time. The hut was used as a tool-shed. Lawther and the gravedigger deposited the coffin.

It is at this point that a number of conflicting accounts of the facts must give way to a little speculation on our part. Lawther invited Fitzsimons and Spence for a drink. The logical course would have been to treat the gravedigger *after* the burial.

So why did Lawther offer the drink in advance? One theory is that he wanted to have Spence away from the coffin for as long as possible, and subsequent events bear this out. Spence testified later that he didn't intend burying the child straightaway but wished to go home, have breakfast and change his clothes. Yet Spence knew he was breaking the law and placing his job in jeopardy. The longer he delayed the burial the more chance there was of his clandestine work being observed by another employee of the Belfast Guardians – or indeed by one of the Guardians themselves.

What is certain is that Spence and Fitzsimons took Lawther up on his offer of a drink, and the trio set off in search of a public house that was open at that early hour. They stopped at the nearest one, on the outskirts of Belfast: the Bunch of Grapes. It was still shut. They had better luck at the next – Alexander's in Mountpottinger – and it was here that Lawther treated his companions and himself to several glasses of whiskey. He paid the carter, who went on his way, having earned a little extra money – and a bottle of stout – for an easy task. The gravedigger left Lawther drinking in the pub and set off home, to have breakfast and change into his workclothes.

By the time Spence got back to the cemetery it was some minutes after noon. The little coffin had lain in the porter's lodge for more than four hours. Lawther had contrived to have the maximum amount of time elapse before his dead infant was committed to the earth. I believe that this was no accident.

In any event Spence set about preparing the grave. He inspected Mrs McCracken's family plot and returned to the porter's lodge to fetch a spade. He was startled to hear low moans coming from the diminutive coffin Lawther had placed there. He put his ear to it.

The baby was still alive.

Spence's reaction to this grisly discovery was bizarre. Rather than open the coffin – and perhaps save the child's life by doing so – he instead hailed a cab and went to the address the widow had given him: 55 Abbot Street. There he found the 'client', John Lawther, and his wife Jane. Spence noted that Lawther was very much the worse for drink; evidently the whiskeys taken at Alexander's hadn't been enough for him. It was two p.m. Spence confronted the husband.

'What was yon that you brought to me in the grave-yard?' he demanded. 'The child is alive!'

Lawther was lost for words. Jane was not. She knew the gravedigger had discovered the awful secret. She flew into a rage and rounded on her husband.

'You *toot*,' she cried. 'Why didn't you bury it yourself?'

'I left it over to this man,' Lawther told her sheepishly.

Spence was in no doubt as to who wore the trousers in the Lawther household. Clearly John had been an unwilling instrument of his wife and mother-in-law. No wonder he'd been drinking so much.

William Spence should have alerted the authorities at this point. He did not; he could not, because he was already guilty of an illegal act – he'd taken possession of a corpse without a burial order from the Guardians. His hands were dirty and he was determined that no more dirt – literally – would be on them that day. If Jane Lawther wanted her child buried then her husband could do the wicked deed.

Lawther had little choice. The evidence of the crime was still in the porter's lodge and it was only a matter of time before somebody discovered it. The carter was long gone and Lawther could hardly engage a cabdriver to return the coffin to his home.

The gravedigger engaged another cab to bring them to Knock Burial Ground. *En route* he explained to Lawther what he'd heard: 'something like a wee moan' emanating from the coffin.

'What are you going to do about it?' Spence asked. 'It's plain that the child is alive.'

'I would certify to you', the drunken man replied, 'that it's been dead since Saturday.'

'Are you going to bury it?'

'Yes.'

On arrival at the cemetery the two men went to the porter's lodge. The moaning coming from the little coffin was more audible than ever. Lawther couldn't fail to hear it, yet he said to Spence: 'There is nothing wrong with it that neither you nor I are to know.'

'I won't bury it,' the gravedigger repeated, and a fierce argument ensued. Spence refused to have anything more to do with the dreadful business and would not open the McCracken family plot. He told Lawther there was some freshly dug earth in a remote corner of the cemetery. Spence had been clearing some ground there with a view to making extra plots; Knock Burial Ground had all but exhausted its capacity by 1884 and the Guardians were seeking to extend it.

Lawther brought out the tiny coffin and carried it to the place Spence indicated. There he found the half-dug grave. While Spence watched in silent horror, the drunken father dumped the coffin in without ceremony and filled in the hole with his hands, covering the coffin with five or six inches of soil. He extended a dirty hand for Spence to take.

'Here,' he said. 'And I hope there'll be nothing more about this matter.'

Spence knew his meaning. The secret would be safe with him. He shook Lawther's hand.

'All right,' he said. 'There'll be nothing more about it.'

They engaged yet another cab to bring them back to the city. Spence left Lawther to further drown his sorrows at the Bunch of Grapes and continued home on foot. It was now five-thirty and night was approaching.

William Spence sat for a time in his kitchen, brooding. The effects of the whiskey he'd drunk before breakfast had worn off and he was beginning to appreciate the enormity of the crime he'd been a silent witness to. His conscience was troubling him.

He had to talk to somebody. His sister lived nearby and he decided to confide in her husband, David Robinson.

Robinson was sympathetic to his brother-in-law's plight. He agreed to help. They went first to the home of Jane McCracken and explained the situation. The widow refused to believe that the infant was still alive. Spence offered to bring her to the cemetery and so confirm it. She declined. Her daughter, she told the men, was ill and needed her.

Spence knew this was untrue; he'd seen the daughter

earlier that afternoon and she'd looked to be the picture of health.

The gravedigger and Robinson arrived at the cemetery at around eight o'clock, when night had fallen. By this time the child had lain under the earth for three hours or more. Spence fetched a spade from the shed, Robinson lit a lantern, and they made for the spot where Lawther had buried the infant with his bare hands. Spence threw back the soil and set his spade under the coffin. He carried it back to the porter's lodge and shut the door.

'Is it alive?' Robinson asked.

Spence put an ear to the lid. He nodded. He could hear the same low moaning coming from the coffin. Lawther had indeed buried a living, breathing child.

Here the story takes another bizarre turn. We have two men in a shed with a coffin they know contains a living infant. The infant could die at any moment; it's been in the coffin at least since dawn – and has lain for hours under the cold earth as well. The porter's lodge is a tool-shed with, to hand, any number of implements that could be used to prise off the coffin lid, screwed down as it is in only two places. The end of a spade could do the job with ease.

What do the men do? They leave the child imprisoned and dying, and depart for the home of a local man, James McFadden, to seek his counsel.

McFadden, a farmer who lived across the way from the cemetery, must have thought he was dealing with a couple of halfwits: two strong men who seemed incapable of opening a flimsy little coffin. But he grabbed a screwdriver nevertheless and returned with them to the Knock Burial Ground.

By some miracle the child had survived its ordeal. On

opening the coffin with McFadden's screwdriver, Spence saw that the infant was breathing. Its little eyes were shut, it was moaning, and its skin had a deathly pallor.

The men brought the child, still in its coffin, to the home of John Gelston, another local farmer. Gelston's wife examined it. The child, she noted, was 'dressed like other children dead', with 'plenty of wadding around it'. It was as cold as ice. She wrapped the unfortunate creature in a blanket and placed it near the kitchen fire for warmth. It began to move its hands. Spence went to fetch Dr Irvine, the Knock GP; when they returned to the farmhouse the child had opened its eyes and Mrs Gelston was giving it a little warm and sweetened milk.

There was not much Irvine could do. He calculated that the baby had been in the coffin for fourteen or fifteen hours. He left it in Mrs Gelston's care. It died at about one in the morning.

Spence in the meantime had decided to come clean about the affair, if only to save himself. He went to the Royal Irish Constabulary in Strandtown, told his tale, and two officers visited the Lawthers' home at 11.15 on the Monday night.

They found there a distraught and very drunken John Lawther and his mother-in-law Mrs McCracken. The sergeant promptly arrested them, and inquired after the whereabouts of Jane Lawther, the child's mother. The widow informed him that her daughter was in 'a somewhat delicate state of health' and resting upstairs. This seemed to satisfy the sergeant; he left Jane alone and had her mother and husband conveyed to Strandtown, where they were charged with wilful murder.

An inquest held the following day in Knock threw

some light on the circumstances surrounding the horrific episode. Dr Irvine had enlisted the help of his colleague Dr Croker in carrying out a post-mortem examination on the dead infant. The cause of death was not hard to establish: suffocation compounded with exposure.

The physicians discovered that Mrs McCracken had lied. The baby hadn't been born prematurely; it had 'come to its proper time'. It was, however, not a normal child. Its body was quite large in proportion to the head; so large, in fact, that it barely fitted in the coffin.

There was moreover a tumour on the spine and the spine itself was crooked. The doctors doubted that a child born with such deformities would have lived for very long.

This, then, was the motive behind the murder. Jane Lawther had no wish to nurse a baby that was doomed anyway.

But had she attempted to hasten its death? It did not appear so; the doctors examined the stomach but found no trace of poison. There were no indications of violence. Jane and her mother had simply confined the baby to a coffin and allowed it to die a 'natural' death.

When the case came to trial on 16 December 1884, the court was well attended; the act of brutality had sent shockwaves through Belfast.

Gravedigger Spence had been fired by the Guardians. He was fortunate not to be convicted of being an accessory to murder, and his alerting of the police must have counted in his favour. Nevertheless several of the jurors were astonished at his laxity when he knew that a live infant was lying under the soil of Knock Burial Ground.

The two women, under cross-examination, began to

dig their own graves, as it were – they each gave testimony that conflicted with that of other witnesses. First there was the question of the day on which the actual birth of the child had taken place. A neighbour, Elizabeth McCann, claimed to have met Mrs McCracken on 3 November, and learned that her daughter Jane had given birth to a son on Hallowe'en – two weeks prior to the date given by the widow in her testimony. McCann had enquired after the baby's health and was told it had been born 'broken-backed'. She added that no doctor had seen it at the time.

McCann stated further that she'd spoken to Jane Lawther some days before the baby was born and heard that Jane had had a fall from a tram. The accident *could* have led to deformity in the baby. However, the doctors who'd carried out the post-mortem had concluded that the 'injury to the spine was congenital malformation'. The child had appeared otherwise healthy.

The defence lawyers cited Dr Croker's findings in an attempt to clear the two women and the luckless Mr Lawther. Croker had suggested that prolonged pressure on the tumour on the baby's spine might have led to 'como', and that a person without medical knowledge might not have been able to tell the difference between a comatose baby and a dead one. The judge, Chief Justice Murphy, dismissed this and urged the jury to return a verdict of wilful murder.

The jury obliged. They decided that all three – mother, daughter and son-in-law – were guilty of manslaughter, yet recommended mercy. Although this lesser charge carried with it a more lenient penalty than that of murder, the jurors were reluctant to subject the two women – the elderly widow in particular – to the mandatory sentence of ten years' penal servitude.

Murphy did not share the jury's sense of compassion. He wished to impose the maximum sentence.

'John Lawther, Jane Lawther and Jane McCracken,' he said, 'you have, on very clear and cogent evidence, been found guilty of this terrible crime. I cannot, for my part, see any distinction between you. It is hard, in my mind, to say which of you is most guilty.'

He addressed the accused in turn, beginning with Jane McCracken.

'You, the grandmother,' he said, 'that arranged all for this business with the gravedigger when you heard that your grandchild – as you must have heard – was moaning in the coffin, you would not stir hand or foot in order to strive and rescue it from its terrible fate.'

Next the Lawthers received a tongue-lashing.

'For you, Lawther, the father that carried this child out to a premature tomb, or for you, terrible woman – a scandal to your sex – who upbraided your too-timid husband because he did not resolutely carry out the terrible fate you had fixed for this child, how to limit the punishment I don't know. The law has fixed it at ten years' penal servitude, and that would be my sentence forthwith upon you, were it not that the jury have added – I know not upon what grounds – such recommendations, though certainly it startled and astounded me to see it here.'

It will surely never be known why the three decided to bury the child alive – or whose decision it was. They could have chosen a somewhat more humane course and perhaps administered poison, as the doctors suspected they might have. Anything would have been preferable to the ordeal the baby underwent.

We should not rule out the possibility that all three

were reluctant to break the fifth commandment in a direct way. They may have believed that *allowing* the infant to die was not, in the eyes of God, the same as murder.

The law ruled otherwise. If Jane Lawther, her mother and her husband thought the judge might be persuaded to show true clemency, they were mistaken. Their crime of attempting to bury a child alive had upset him deeply. He shaved a bare two years from the maximum sentence permitted. All were given eight years of penal servitude in Crumlin Road prison.

Jane Reynolds and the Ice-cream Vendor's Wife

Giuseppe Mezza was the first of the family to make the journey to Ireland. He came from Pozzuoli, the charming village to the north of Naples that would one day be the birthplace of Sophia Loren. Mezza, who'd later anglicize his first name to Joseph, brought with him the secret that had been in his family since the seventeenth century: the making of delicious ice-cream.

He set up shop in Belfast in 1907, unsure about the reception the Irish would give his wares. He was not disappointed: within a year Joe Mezza's Ice Cream Parlour was doing so well that Giuseppe invited six other members of his extended family to join him and his wife. His second cousin, Angelo di Lucia, aged twenty-seven, made the move in 1911. By this time Belfast had more Italian ice-cream shops than were strictly necessary, so Angelo looked elsewhere for suitable premises. He found them, and moved to Sligo town the following year.

The enterprise proved immensely successful. Before long Angelo's shop in Ratcliffe Street was a fixture in the town and he himself a 'character' whom the townspeople – the children in particular – welcomed into their midst and into their hearts.

The only blot on Angelo's landscape was his wife Rosa. To be sure, she was pretty, warm and generous – yet she did not fit in with Angelo's ambitions. He wanted a wife who'd 'front' the ice-cream shop as he did, be as outgoing with the Sligo people as he was. Such a wife was good for business.

Alas, Rosa could not – or would not – learn English. By June 1914 she'd been in the country nearly three years and knew only enough of the language to enable her to fill an order and say 'Thank you'. Moreover Rosa didn't share her husband's liking for the social life, preferring to stay at home and take care of the children. There were two by this time – both girls – and a third was on the way.

When seventeen-year-old Jane Reynolds came into Angelo di Lucia's life she came as a godsend. She came in answer to his call for a childminder-cum-shop assistant.

Jane was very satisfactory in the first role. She was the second-eldest girl in a family of eleven children living in Ballymote, a town some thirteen miles due south of Sligo. She was good with children, having acted as a mother to the three youngest of her siblings. Rosa took to her right away. As did Angelo's young brother Pasquali. He was Jane's age.

But Jane Reynolds really came into her own in the ice-cream shop. She had the stunning, dark-eyed looks of a younger Rosa, and she liked people. It wasn't long before Angelo realized what an asset he had in her. His business thrived with Jane behind the counter.

Pasquali di Lucia was as fond as his elder brother of socializing. Very soon he was escorting Jane to dances and taking her to the pictures. But it was innocent fun. In reality Jane and Angelo were having an affair. At first the elder brother tagged along when Pasquali and Jane went out together; later Angelo escorted Jane alone.

In the meantime Rosa di Lucia was having a difficult pregnancy. Angelo did little to alleviate her discomfort. In fact his behaviour towards his wife began to deteriorate from the moment Jane and he became lovers. We have it on the authority of a visitor to the house that Angelo had beaten Rosa the day before she gave birth. On asking Jane the reason, the visitor was told: 'The boss has been after giving a few thumps to her for not peeling potatoes. He has neither love nor liking for his wife.'

The truth of the matter was that Angelo, the boss, was planning on ridding himself of Rosa for good.

She must have known about the affair. Angelo and Jane were in each other's company practically twenty-four hours a day. She shared the work of the ice-cream parlour with him, and shared the house on the first floor with the whole family. Though Rosa understood little English, word must have got back to her that her husband was entertaining Jane more often than was decent. He was a well-known figure in Sligo; he could hardly make a move without half the town knowing about it.

We also have the testimony of Rosa's brother, Joe Mezzo; this indicates that she knew about Jane and her husband. Apparently on the Wednesday, the day after Rosa gave birth, she'd asked Angelo to fetch a glass of water for her.

'No,' he said, 'I won't give you water. I'll give you broth.'

Rosa refused it; she wanted water because she was running a fever. She felt she was dying.

'If I die,' she said, 'you won't wait a month until you marry again.'

Angelo assured her he'd never marry again, and that she wasn't going to die.

Matters came to a head later that day. Rosa's condition worsened and the GP, Dr PJ Flanagan, was called in. He diagnosed neuralgia coupled with 'puerperal insanity'. This is a condition once prevalent in women after childbirth, owing to the absence of aseptic techniques during delivery. It's rarely seen in Ireland nowadays because of the widespread use of antiseptics. It's usually called puerperal fever because the infection leads to a sharp rise in body temperature and sweating. The sufferer experiences hallucinations and an acute thirst.

The following day a nurse arrived to help Rosa with the baby. She noted the woman's feverish condition and spoke to Jane Reynolds. On no account must Rosa be left alone, she advised.

Angelo's reaction to this was to move into his brother Pasquali's bedroom, requesting Jane to share Rosa's bed. The girl would be on hand should his wife's condition deteriorate further. Although it was probably better having another female keeping a watchful eye on Rosa and the infant, it was nevertheless an odd arrangement to come to.

Odder still was the conversation Angelo had with Jane six days later, when he took her aside in the kitchen.

'Jane,' he said, 'my wife's head is gone. Will you kill her for me?'

Just like that. Not surprisingly, Jane was astonished. It was true that Mrs di Lucia was behaving queerly. She would not remain in her sickbed but was up and about at every opportunity, doing unnecessary chores and generally getting under everybody's feet.

But Jane recovered quickly. She too saw the advantage

of having Rosa out of the way, permanently.

'I couldn't do the likes', she said, 'without someone to help me.'

'I'll help you if you start it,' Angelo assured her. 'I'll tell you what to do. You go and get a naggin of whiskey and it will give you great courage and you will be that strong.'

'I haven't the nerve to do it, no matter how strong I am.'

'You'll be strong enough if you take the whiskey,' Angelo pressed, 'and I will marry you when it's done.'

Was there ever a stranger proposal made? Jane took the bait. She decided to put the plan into effect that very night.

A hammer was to be the weapon of death. That was the first mistake Jane made. She could have tried to make the murder look like an accident or, failing that, devise a means by which suspicion might fall on an intruder. Hammers have the annoying tendency to leave clearly identifiable marks. . . .

Rosa was not having a good night. The baby was unusually active, remaining awake and bawling until well after midnight. Jane brought it nearer the bedroom fire and rocked it gently in its cradle, trying to get the infant to sleep. Its crying prevented Rosa from sleeping as well, and she left her bed to fetch more baby clothes, thinking the extra warmth might do the trick. The puerperal fever was causing her to behave more and more oddly.

But the fever had also given Angelo's wife a dreadful thirst. She left her bed again, went downstairs and drank four bottles of lemonade. She was considerate enough to bring one back for Jane. But the girl refused it. This angered Rosa and she flung the contents of the bottle into Jane's face.

So far, this is Jane's version of events. We don't find out what it was that provoked Rosa into throwing the lemonade. Why was she angry? It may well have been a desperate and unhappy woman's response to the object of her husband's lust. She may even have confronted Jane with her knowledge of the affair – and Jane may have decided that now was the best time to do the evil deed.

'Go back to bed, Mrs di Lucia,' she ordered. 'The doctor will be vexed and won't want to see you again.'

'Not at all,' Rosa answered. The phrase was one of the few bits of English she had.

The sick woman put the latch on the bedroom door, went to the cradle and covered the baby's face with the sheet. Then she joined Jane in the bed. By six o'clock she'd finally drifted off to sleep.

Jane remained awake for another hour. By this time Rosa was sleeping soundly. She went downstairs to the little utility room where Angelo kept his tools and returned with a clawhammer concealed in a dishcloth. She tapped softly on the door of Pasquali's room. Angelo, wide awake too, opened it.

'What'll I do now?' the girl whispered.

'Stuff the dishcloth in her mouth. That way nobody will hear her.'

Jane returned to the darkened room. Soft snoring told her that Rosa was sound asleep. She unwrapped the hammer. Her intended victim's mouth was wide open.

Swiftly Jane followed Angelo's advice. Gripping the hammer in one hand she thrust the cloth into Rosa's mouth. The woman awoke at once.

She was the stronger of the two. They fought. Rosa

grabbed a handful of Jane's hair and got a hold on the hammer.

What happened next remains a mystery. Jane insisted later that Rosa had wrenched the hammer from her grasp and, in doing so, struck herself accidentally on the forehead. This may have been the case. It may also be true that Jane got in that first blow. In any event the struggles and cries of the two women alerted Angelo. He rushed into the room and found them fighting on the bed. Rosa was lying on top of Jane.

Angelo came up from behind. He wrenched the hammer out of his wife's hand. Thrusting his fingers into her nostrils, he yanked her head back and struck her on the head with the hammer. Two blows were sufficient: Rosa collapsed unconscious on the floor.

Jane was squatting on the bed, vomiting. When it came to killing she really didn't have the stomach for it – that much at least can be said in her defence.

But she made her second mistake then, and Angelo behaved equally stupidly. Rosa lay unconscious with a fractured skull. There was severe bleeding. Now was the time to make up a plausible story, perhaps involving a burglar whom Rosa had surprised.

Instead Angelo and Jane lifted Rosa and placed her on the bed. Jane fetched water and together they washed the blood from the head. Angelo removed his wife's stained nightdress and dressed her in a fresh one. Next he wound a cloth around her head to cover the wounds and tied it with a bandage. Jane, having cleaned the bed, helped him put Rosa back between the covers.

She was not dead by that time, but dying. It was close to seven o'clock.

Angelo roused his brother Pasquali and told him that

Rosa had had an accident. He wanted a priest. Pasquali was a superstitious youth and refused to remain in the house, therefore Angelo sent Jane with him.

At 8.10 they returned with Canon Doorly and went up to the room where Rosa lay.

'She was lying on the bed with her head bandaged,' Doorly recalled. 'The bandages were in such a position as to conceal the wounds to her forehead. Her husband was in the room and seemed to be in great grief. He was on his knees by the bed. I asked him to leave.'

The canon had been called in to administer extreme unction. He went to the bedside to begin the ceremony.

'I thought she looked very much alive,' he remembered. 'I touched her cheek to see whether she was hot or cold and she seemed quite warm. I thought she might be semiconscious or something like that, and that I could anoint her. I proceeded to do so.'

He first asked Jane Reynolds to remove the bandage from around Rosa's head; it covered her forehead entirely. Doorly saw one of the ugly wounds, the smallest one. He asked about it.

'I was left to mind her,' Jane said, 'but I fell asleep and I don't know what happened to her.'

Canon Doorly left the house in Ratcliffe Street in a troubled frame of mind. He'd given the last sacrament to a seemingly unconscious woman and he didn't know whether she was alive or dead. Neither the woman's husband nor brother-in-law could tell him how she'd sustained the injury. He decided to alert the police.

Angelo di Lucia was arrested at his home at ten a.m. on 9 December 1914, and charged with the murder of his wife. The hammer – which, inexplicably, was still in the room – was removed as evidence.

At about the same time, Jane Reynolds was standing on the platform at Sligo railway station, waiting for the train that would take her to her home in Ballymote. She was approached by two police officers. One was Head Constable Sean Murphy. He spoke quietly to the girl and ushered her into the waiting-room, there to take her statement. He placed her under arrest.

The doctor who examined the remains left the coroner in no doubt that Rosa had been murdered. Dr Thomas Rouse found head wounds which had caused a depressed fracture of the skull. His verdict was that Rosa died of shock following concussion. Death was probably not instantaneous, he concluded. It was likely there was a period of unconsciousness, probably lasting several hours.

Dr PJ Flanagan, who'd attended Rosa before and after the birth of her child, stated that the last time he'd seen her she'd been on the road to recovery. Patrick Quinn, the coroner, asked him to describe the condition of the body. Was it a case of suicide?

'In my opinion the wounds could not have been self-inflicted,' the doctor said. 'They could have been produced by the hammer. I actually compared it with the wounds, and the curved wound corresponds in size with the curve on the head of the hammer. The other wounds corresponded more or less with the head of the hammer and were produced by some such weapon.'

He was asked about the rest of the port-mortem findings – in particular the condition and contents of Rosa's stomach.

'The deceased could not have taken four bottles of lemonade three or four hours before her death, without there being some trace of it,' was his verdict.

There was also the matter of the naggin of whiskey. Jane claimed she'd drunk it before the murder but the police found that the bottle hadn't been touched. Jane had had no need of Dutch courage. All things pointed to the cold-blooded and cowardly slaying of a sick woman.

Jane and Angelo languished in Sligo Prison for nearly a year before their case came to court. There was a reason for the long delay. At first it was planned to try the pair in Sligo but Angelo's solicitor had intervened. There was a complication: Jane was pregnant by Angelo.

The news reached the people of the town – and they were shocked. Anger welled up against the thirty-year-old Italian who'd seduced a country girl of seventeen, and had perhaps persuaded her to help murder his wife.

Jane gave birth to the child in July 1915 while still in remand custody. The authorities agreed that it might not be a good idea to try Angelo before a jury of Sligomen. It was therefore arranged that he appear before the King's Bench, Dublin, on 2 November. There would be two trials – first Jane's, then Angelo's. Because each had given a statement that contradicted the other's, they could not be arraigned together; the law prohibited their testifying against each other.

Jane appeared in court with her four-month-old baby in her arms, a pathetic figure who at once won the sympathy of the women in the public gallery. A female warder took charge of the infant and Jane entered her plea: not guilty. She appeared calm and self-possessed.

Opening the trial for the prosecution, John Gordon pointed out Jane's third fatal error: nobody – not Jane, not Angelo, not Pasquali – had bothered to ask how Rosa had sustained her wounds, nor had they made any effort to tell anybody about the incident. They'd simply let her perish.

Jane must be guilty of murder, Gordon went on, because Angelo and she had gone to great lengths to remove all traces of the blood – Angelo had even burned Rosa's incriminating nightdress. She'd died after receiving three hammer blows to the head, any one of which could have caused death.

He called Pasquali di Lucia first. The youth told the court how he'd been woken early in the morning of 9 December 1914 by Rosa's cries of 'Oh, oh, oh!' He'd roused his brother.

'The missus is gone a little bit in the head,' Angelo had informed him.

'Were you not sufficiently curious to enquire what was wrong?' Gordon asked.

'No.'

'What did you do then?'

'I went to sleep.'

'And you heard nothing more?'

'No.'

It was plausible enough but the jury looked unsatisfied with Pasquali's testimony.

Mrs Tiernan, the maternity nurse who'd attended Rosa, was up next. She told the court how Jane had called on her later that same morning to tell her that her 'missus is dead'. The girl said that when she'd called out to Rosa at about 6 a.m. to give her a drink of water she'd got no reply. She'd turned round to face her and saw that the blanket was drawn up over her head.

'What did she do then?' Gordon wanted to know.

'She said that she drew back the blanket,' the nurse told the court, 'and saw the cut on her forehead and the hammer lying in the bed beside her.'

'What was the prisoner's response to that?'

'She said that the missus must have killed herself.'

Nurse Tiernan stated that she'd gone to the house in Ratcliffe Street and seen the dead woman.

'Can you describe the condition in which you found the deceased?' Gordon asked.

'She was lying in her bed with a bandage around her head. There was a mark on her forehead, another between her eyes, and a third on her temple.'

'Did you notice anything else?'

'I did. The sheet and Mrs di Lucia's night clothing had been changed.' When cross-examined, the nurse declared that, in her opinion, the bedclothes couldn't have been changed by one person – not if Rosa had been lying in the bed at the time.

It is a curious thing about the hammer – the most incriminating piece of evidence – that it appears to have meandered from one place to another that morning. The next witness, the police sergeant who'd arrested Angelo di Lucia, claimed to have seen it lying beside the hearth.

Apparently Angelo had made as many stupid mistakes as Jane had. He may have burned Rosa's stained nightdress, yet Sergeant Reilly found the bedsheet in the bathroom. It was soaked with blood. He also found the naggin bottle of whiskey – untouched – on the kitchen table.

Jane's plea of not guilty was becoming untenable. Dr Flanagan told the court that Rosa's wounds couldn't have been self-inflicted. Moreover the hammer blows need not necessarily have been delivered by a powerful person.

'Would the accused have been capable of delivering such blows?' Gordon wished to know.

'Yes,' said the GP.

Jane Reynolds was not required to give evidence. There was no need: the statement taken at the railway station by Head Constable Murphy was incriminating enough. Her counsel, Fitzgerald Kenny, objected to its being read out in court, claiming that it had not been offered voluntarily. The judge overruled the objection and admitted the statement as evidence.

The court heard how Angelo had induced Jane to kill Rosa with the hammer; how she'd hesitated; how Angelo had persuaded her that drinking the naggin of whiskey would strengthen her resolve; how she'd bungled the murder and how Angelo had finished the job.

Kenny tried to convince the jury that a girl of seventeen was incapable of such a violent crime. And, although it was claimed that Jane had fought with Rosa for possession of the hammer, the doctor who'd examined her hadn't found a mark on her.

The jurors retired – but returned a half hour later with a question. What, the foreman wondered, was Jane's position if she'd been present when Angelo murdered his wife yet had taken no part in it? The judge assured them that, by consenting to murder, Jane would be equally guilty.

The jury returned a second time. Yes, they'd decided that Jane Reynolds was guilty but nevertheless recommended clemency. The judge rejected this plea. He sentenced her to be hanged at Sligo Prison on 2 December. She broke down.

'Oh, I didn't do it, my lord!' she cried. 'He killed his wife. I have a little child!'

This was too much for many women in the public gallery; they burst into tears as the prisoner was taken down below.

Angelo di Lucia was tried the following day. The case for the prosecution was very strong. A man finds his wife dying from head injuries and doesn't seek help, doesn't even rouse anybody else in the house. Instead he bandages her head, changes her nightdress and the sheets, and returns to bed.

And why didn't he ask Jane how it had happened? Because there was a clear case of collusion. Jane knew all about it and was furthermore a party to it.

Angelo's counsel tried to make the best of a bad lot. Pasquali once again gave evidence about hearing Rosa's screams while his brother was asleep. Surely this pointed to the possibility that Angelo's wife was already dead before her husband left his bed.

Not so, said the prosecutor. After Angelo was roused by Jane's knock on the door, he'd been absent from Pasquali's room for up to an hour before Jane had come to tell Pasquali that Rosa was dead. What had Angelo been up to during that time?

Angelo and Jane, he continued, had imagined that they could pass off Rosa's death as one from natural causes. But the canon had put paid to that: he'd seen the wound. The pair had then suggested suicide. It didn't wash.

The jury agreed and, after only thirty minutes, returned with a verdict of guilty. The judge set Angelo's date of execution for the same day as Jane's.

Neither sentence was carried out. Because of her age at the time of the murder, clemency was shown to Jane and her sentence commuted to life imprisonment. She served three years and was released on condition that she enter a convent – a choice, or indeed a fate, once reserved for many of Ireland's convicted female killers.

And Angelo? He cheated the gallows too – and in a

curious way he had Jane Reynolds to thank for this. On 23 November, three weeks after his conviction, his death sentence was commuted to life imprisonment. It was felt that since two were involved in the murder it would be perverse to hang the one and not the other.

He served eleven years of his sentence in Sligo Prison, was released in 1927 and deported back to his homeland. There he rejoined his family. Pasquali and his three nieces had left Ireland early in 1916, not long after Angelo's conviction. They couldn't live with the shame, the dark shadow cast by a man who'd seduced a girl of seventeen and induced her to assist him in the savage slaying of his wife.

Mary Moynihan, the Resentful Servant from Kanturk

Jeremiah Horgan farmed a modest property of eleven acres in the parish of Toureenvouscane, Kanturk, County Cork. His earnings enabled him and his wife to employ three servants: two boys, and a girl whom they'd hired in 1918. She was fifteen at the time. She didn't stretch the family purse; Mary Moynihan's weekly wage would be the equivalent of £20 in today's money. Admittedly she also got room and board, but the work was hard, as it was for any servant girl in the rural Ireland of the time.

The Horgans were childless. When Jeremiah set out for Cork city early on the morning of 9 September 1922, he took with him one of the servant lads, leaving three people in the farmhouse: his wife Nora, the other servant boy, and Mary Moynihan. By ten o'clock the two women were alone; the lad left behind had gone off to the creamery with the churns of milk.

Horgan had pigs to sell at the market. By three in the afternoon he'd disposed of them all and set off on the return journey. On his arrival home he received terrible news from a neighbour. Nora was dead, murdered in her own kitchen by a stranger.

The other servant boy was on hand to tell Horgan of the aftermath. His wife's body had been conveyed to the police station in Kanturk. The local GP, John Joe O'Riordan, could be found there, the neighbour explained, as could Mary Moynihan, who'd been present at the time of the murder. Horgan jumped aboard his cart and whipped the horse into a gallop.

The servant girl had already given a statement by the time Horgan reached the police station. It read as follows.

> About half nine this morning Mrs Horgan was plucking a fowl in the scullery and I heard some talk. Mrs Horgan called 'Mary!' and on entering the scullery I saw a tall young man of the tramp class dressed in brown with Mrs Horgan. I ran to Mrs Horgan and both of them fell.
>
> The man pulled me away, struck me on the head and I fell. Mrs Horgan called me again and when she got up the man put her on her knees and told her that if she made any alarm he'd kill her. The man then disappeared. I went to take Mrs Horgan out into the air but found she was dead. I didn't see anything in the man's hand.

It was a simple statement made by a simple, uneducated country girl of nineteen. It was good enough for the local members of the Civic Guard and good enough for Jeremiah Horgan. His wife had been brutally murdered.

What Mary's statement failed to explain were the wounds. Dr O'Riordan had examined the corpse and declared that Nora had died from a compound fracture of the skull. He counted nine wounds in all and decided that they'd been inflicted by 'some sharp instrument and not given with great force'.

Coroner Ryan concurred when an inquest was held on the Monday. A verdict of 'wilful murder against some person unknown' was returned. Nora Horgan was laid to rest. The matter itself was not.

While the wake was in full swing, two neighbours calling at the house had seen a man and a woman standing in the shadows in the yard. They were kissing. The neighbours identified the pair as Jeremiah Horgan and Mary Moynihan.

Time passed. Mary left the Horgan farm the day after the funeral and returned to her parents' home near Bandon. The servant boys stayed on. By chance one of them found a letter lying open on the kitchen table. It was from Mary to Horgan. The lad was surprised to see that Mary had addressed her former employer as 'Dear Jerry', an unheard of liberty, given the strict hierarchy that governed country life. It induced him to read on.

'Jerry,' Mary had written, 'you know in your heart I would not harm you. I know the talk of the people is frightful but they can prove nothing against me. It was always told to me that all would come out after a time. I am going to stick to what I said. Hoping it will be all known soon, please God.'

The boy made enquiries. He learned that a brother of the deceased had brought a letter from Horgan to Mary. Hers was by way of reply. Then one thing led to another, people began to talk and compare notes, and before very long the neighbours who'd seen Horgan and Mary kissing on the evening of the wake were telling their story to all who'd listen. Could it be, some wondered, that either

Horgan or the girl – or both – had wanted Nora Horgan dead?

The Guards were notified. Superintendent Sean Fahy of Cork came to investigate, and talked to a number of local people. The suspicions raised by the letter were confirmed: Mary and her employer had been conducting an affair. The letter also seemed to suggest that Mary had had some part in the murder. Nora had been found dead in her arms, and the police had only Mary's word that a stranger had been involved. She made a second statement, again implicating a stranger, yet when Fahy asked her to elaborate, she replied by saying, 'Put me no questions. I cannot answer.'

Fahy arrested her and charged her with murder.

The case was a long time coming to trial: it finally opened on 11 December 1924 – more than two years after the murder – at the Central Criminal Court, Dublin.

Mary pleaded not guilty. The trouble was that every statement she made was at variance with the last. Now the man in brown 'of the tramp class' was replaced by another suspect: Daniel Kiely, the local postman.

Kiely was called to the witness box. His testimony proved that it would have been physically impossible for him to have murdered Nora Horgan: he was delivering the post many miles away at the time – and two other witness supported this. 'The reflection cast upon his [Kiely's] name is a foul injustice,' said one, referring to Mary's accusation. She hastily withdrew it.

The prosecutor, Joseph Carrigan, called as a witness the first man on the scene: Jack O'Connor. He was passing the Horgan house with two neighbours, Daniel Cronin and Ellen Clifford, when they heard cries for help coming from the direction of the front-door.

'What was the nature of these cries?' Carrigan asked.

'It sounded like, "Nora, Nora Fitz, will you come to me."'

'Did the accused say anything when you entered the house?'

'Yes. She said, "Oh dear God, Jack and I alone!"'

'Did you not think that was an unusual thing to say?' Carrigan asked.

O'Connor admitted that it was. He went on to tell the court that Mary's explanation to him was more or less the same as that given in her first statement. She'd been doing some washing in the kitchen. She'd seen a strange man enter the scullery and strike Nora Horgan. She had also said another odd thing to O'Connor: 'He swore me not to tell who he was; not to tell he was a man.'

O'Connor had found the dead woman in Mary's arms in the scullery. He'd observed, he said, 'all the signs of butchery'. Nora's head was a mass of wounds; the blood had become encrusted and had ceased flowing.

Dr O'Riordan, who examined the body some time later, concluded that the nine wounds had been inflicted by a slasher, or circular saw, found in the house. There was also a car spring, bloodied, that may or may not have been used. Altogether the murder was a savage act of barbarism.

It was the turn of the defence counsel to question the doctor. He asked whether O'Riordan believed that the murder was the work of a woman. He did not.

If Mary Moynihan was as innocent as she claimed to be, and the doctor was convinced the murderer was male, then a motive had to be considered.

Mary had described the stranger in the brown suit as a tramp; it was possible that Nora had insulted or wronged such a person at one time and that the man sought vengeance. Or he might have intended robbing the house and Nora had surprised him.

Yet as the trial progressed it was becoming more and more obvious that Horgan himself had been involved in some way. This is not to say he was the murderer – he was in Cork at the time and had many witnesses to prove it, including the lad who'd accompanied him to the fair.

Carrigan cross-examined Horgan. What had Mary Moynihan told him about the murder of his wife?

'She said that a strange man in brown clothes came in and killed her.'

'And what did you say to that?'

'I said I wouldn't let the case go like that; that there'd be more about it.'

Carrigan knew this to be an untruth. There had not been 'more about it'. Had the neighbours not gone to the police, then neither Mary nor anybody else would have been before the court that day.

Mary's counsel, Joseph Healy, questioned Horgan. 'Were relations between your wife and the prisoner friendly?' he asked.

Horgan said they were.

'Did you ever see the prisoner particularly violent?'

'No, I did not.'

Healy wanted to scotch the rumours that Horgan and Mary were lovers. He asked him about the incident on the night of the wake, when he'd been spotted in the yard.

'Did you hear it sworn', he asked, 'that the prisoner embraced you, or that you embraced the prisoner, before the funeral? Is that true?'

'No. I was embracing everybody in the yard that day.'

'And she did not embrace you?'

'No. I wouldn't let her.'

This was a silly statement. Why embrace everybody *except* Mary Moynihan? Especially when they were on such friendly terms that she addressed him as 'Jerry'. It was a lie that Horgan hadn't kissed her. The prosecution called two further witnesses who swore he had. According to one, Mary had returned the embrace, saying: 'Oh dear God, Jerry, what will you do?'

Mary Moynihan was convicted of murder on the second day of her trial. Healy had defended her well, knowing that all the cards were stacked against her. She was a servant girl, after all – a person considered to be of little worth and, above all, an unreliable witness. Rural Cork society – and indeed Irish society as a whole – was strong on class distinction.

Healy demanded of the jury that they produce a motive, should they decide to find her guilty.

'Was it because the prisoner and Jeremiah Horgan were seen to embrace that this girl beat her mistress to death in the most brutal and cold-blooded way?' he asked. 'I submit that that incident did not supply a motive for the crime, and I further contend that a girl like the prisoner could not have killed her mistress, who belonged to the farming class, without receiving a blow, a mark or a bruise in the course of the struggle.'

Then there was the letter Mary had written to Horgan. It was innocence itself, Healy suggested. He asked the jury to consider the meaning of the words, 'Jerry, you know in your heart I would not harm you.'

'What harm could she do two or three months after

the murder,' he asked, 'except by her evidence?'

Healy continued to read. '"It was always told to me that all would come out after a time. . . . Hoping it will be all known soon, please God."'

'Are those the words of a guilty woman?' he asked. 'Would a guilty woman be "hoping it will be all known soon"? Her story is that this murder was committed by a man, and if she told his name, what protection would she be afforded, seeing that there was no police force in Cork at this time? She dared not tell the man's name, except if she wanted to join Nora Horgan in the churchyard.'

Healy was alluding to the fact that in September 1922 the Civil War was being waged with great ferocity. Martial law was in force, and desperadoes of the opposing factions were roaming the countryside. Under the guise of politics many crimes of violence were being committed.

Healy had one last trick up his sleeve. He tried to convince the jury that Jeremiah Horgan was implicated in his wife's death. He'd made a pretence of going to Cork on the fateful day, had slipped back to the farm unseen and murdered her.

Carrigan's response was to sarcastically compliment his opponent on the quality of his defence – and to ridicule Healy's last suggestion. The jury retired to consider their verdict.

They were gone a little over an hour and a half and returned with a verdict of guilty, with a strong recommendation to mercy. As the judge donned the black cap Mary rose and shouted her protest.

'I shielded the man who committed the murder!' she cried. 'I will shield him no longer. The man that will be arrested is Horgan. He committed the murder. He put me in a state that he tempted me with murder as well. He forced me into that and I shielded him at the time. But I won't shield him now!'

Horgan sat immobile in the court as the judge passed sentence of death on Mary. She was to be hanged on 13 January 1925.

She barely escaped the gallows. A farcical situation arose by which an appeal was granted – and set for a date *after* 13 January. The excuse given was that the person who could grant the appeal – the Minister for Justice – was away from his office for the Christmas holidays.

Matters were worked out satisfactorily, however, and the appeal heard while Mary was still alive. The appeal failed. Healy tried again and succeeded. Her sentence was commuted to life.

Did Mary Moynihan do it? Certainly she was guilty of lying. The passers-by who'd answered the call for help swore that the cry had come from the front doorway of the house. The scullery was at the back. When the neighbours entered the scullery, Mary pretended to be weighed down by Nora's corpse, unable to free herself. Who except Mary could have called out from the front-door?

And Horgan? Evidently he and Mary were lovers – or at any rate on highly intimate terms. He claimed to have been on good terms with Nora as well, and the neighbours supported this claim. Yet he'd corresponded with Mary just two months after Nora's death. This was hardly the action of a man who knew her to have murdered his wife.

The man 'of the tramp class' was never found.

Annie Walshe of Fedamore and her Murderous Nephew

On 27 October 1924 *The Irish Times* covered a murder in County Limerick. The report read: 'A man named Edward Walshe, a labourer, was shot dead at Fedamore on Friday night. It appears that at midnight Walshe was in his house when he was fired at and mortally wounded.' The paper went on to say that the Civic Guards at Croom were making inquiries.

The newspaper reader of the time had grown accustomed to such reports. Scarcely a week went by when the papers *didn't* carry news of a shooting somewhere in the country. The Civil War had ended that spring, yet sporadic fighting and 'executions' continued, as old scores were settled among members of pro-Treaty or anti-Partitionist groupings.

The evening after the shooting, Chief Superintendent McGuire of the Limerick police received word that two of his officers were interviewing the dead man's widow. She wished to make a statement and his presence was requested. Annie Walshe's version of events bore out McGuire's initial conjecture that the victim had somehow become embroiled in politics; the shooting had the hallmarks of an execution.

There were three players in the murder the newspapers were to call the 'sordid Croom case'. They were the deceased, his wife, and his nephew, Michael Talbot.

On the face of it there was nothing remarkable about the dead man. Edward Walshe was a farm labourer, sixty years old at the time of the murder. He was poor even by the standards of a labourer of County Limerick in the twenties. His wife and he were rearing six young children in a small shack on less than a half acre of land. They had one cow, a few chickens and very little else. Walshe, the sixth son of a big family, had married late. He was fifty then; Annie Kiernan was twenty. Throughout their ten years of married life the couple knew only a poverty that verged on near-destitution. Annie's sole possession of any value was a wedding ring that had cost £12.

She was unhappy with her life in Fedamore. On marrying Walshe she'd left her family home and had returned only once. The distance wasn't great but Walshe had had a serious falling-out with his in-laws. It could be said that the two families were feuding. Walshe refused to allow a Kiernan into his home and forbade his wife from visiting her own people. Annie grew resentful of the Walshes, her husband most of all; as the years passed the resentment turned to something uglier. Walshe remained unaware of his wife's smouldering hatred.

It was this hatred – rather than politics – that led to his brutal murder. That he was murdered is beyond doubt. What will always remain a mystery, however, is the identity of his killer. There are three conflicting stories to contend with, three separate versions of the events surrounding Edward Walshe's death, and four juries had to choose from them. So must we.

Here, first, is Annie's initial story. She stuck to it (or

most of it anyway) to the very end, blithely disregarding the most glaring discrepancy: she maintained that her husband had been shot. This was patently untrue. Somebody had hatcheted him to death.

It was night, Annie told Chief Superintendent McGuire, and the family were all in bed. A knock had sounded on the door of their cottage. Her husband told her to ignore it.

Their nocturnal visitor was persistent. He knocked again and demanded that the door be opened. Before they had a chance to do so, however, the caller broke the door down and entered. He yelled to Walshe to come out of his bedroom and into the kitchen. Walshe obeyed and Annie followed him, stopping at the door of the children's room and urging them to remain in their beds.

Annie carried a lamp. The intruder ordered her to extinguish it. She refused. He struck her in the face.

'Did you recognize the intruder?' McGuire asked.

'I did not. It was dark. I had no light any more.'

'But you saw him hit your husband with a stick?'

'Yes. Then he shot poor Edward.'

'How many times?'

'Two times, I think. He had a revolver.'

'You saw the revolver?'

'I did,' said Annie.

'In the dark? Did you see the flash of powder?'

'I did.'

McGuire was well aware that Annie's story was a tissue of lies. He could hardly believe the woman could be so stupid as to fabricate such an implausible statement. He knew there'd been no firearm – revolver or otherwise – involved. Edward Walshe's corpse lay in a mortuary in

Croom, and Dr William Hederman had carried out a post-mortem examination. It was incontrovertible that Walshe had been battered to death. There was a small bruise under the right eye, and two huge wounds on the head, either of which would have been sufficient to cause death. They were evidently inflicted by a semi-sharp instrument. Only one part of Annie's story tallied with Hederman's findings: the wound under Walshe's right eye had been caused by a fall.

Chief Superintendent McGuire held a conference in the garda barracks in Croom, and listened carefully to those officers who had their ear to the ground in Fedamore. McGuire learned of strange goings-on that involved a certain Michael Talbot, Walshe's nephew.

In the early hours of Sunday morning Guard Jim Kenny arrested Talbot at his home at Carnane, Fedamore. He made a confession that led to the arrest of Annie Walshe an hour later. A hearing was arranged for the following day. Annie denied all charges.

'I did not kill my husband,' she pleaded. 'I will swear that Michael Talbot was the man who killed my husband. I am prepared to swear it.'

Thus was Chief Superintendent McGuire confronted by another version of Annie's story. As far as he was concerned it was no more plausible than the first.

According to Annie, Michael Talbot had entered the Walshe house on the night of Friday, 24 October. He was brandishing a revolver. He dragged Edward Walshe out into a field and shot him dead.

And why, McGuire wanted to know, had Annie not at once gone to the police about it? Why had she waited until nearly twenty-four hours had elapsed?

Because she feared Walshe's nephew. She feared for

her life, she said. A year prior to the murder Talbot had
come to the house with a gun. Blind drunk, he'd fired
shots at Edward Walshe and assaulted Annie. Walshe had
gone to the Guards at once; Talbot was arrested and
jailed for six months. Not only that, but the court awarded Annie £20 as compensation for the assault on her.

We should keep our eye on the compensation because
it's significant. It was a large sum of money to be awarded
for a common assault. By extended reasoning, there was
a good chance that a court might award a vastly greater
sum to the widow of a murdered man.

Michael Talbot, aged twenty-two, lived alone in a little cottage not far from Annie's house. He was a
'Walshe', but only by marriage, and was the only member
of her husband's family Annie could tolerate. This, at
least, was the impression she gave to the outside world.

The evening after the killing Annie accused Talbot of
being the perpetrator. McGuire dispatched Guards Kenny and Donleavy to take him in for questioning. They
arrived at the cottage shortly before midnight; nobody
answered their knock. But Kenny, on peering through the
kitchen window, saw that the fire had been recently
stoked and that the remains of a hastily abandoned supper lay on the table. He grew suspicious.

The door was on the latch. The Guards entered the
cottage and searched it. They found no weapons, nor did
they expect to. What they did discover was Talbot himself, lying hidden under the rafters.

'I didn't do anything!' he protested. 'It was Annie.'

Guard Kenny assisted him down from his hiding place
and brought him into the kitchen. He asked Talbot if he
wished to make a formal statement. Talbot did so.

'You may arrest Annie as well as me,' he said. 'I didn't kill him. She killed him with the hatchet.'

'What hatchet?' Kenny asked.

'You'll find it near the fire in Walshe's kitchen. There's two of them. She used the biggest one.'

'Tell us what happened.'

'I held his hands.'

'Mr Walshe's?'

'Yes. Annie struck two blows and he died.'

Guard Kenny studied the suspect. Talbot was a bear of a man, standing easily six foot three in his boots; his work-callused hands looked capable of crushing a man's skull. Annie Walshe was a tiny woman. And here was Talbot trying to convince them that she was the one who'd wielded the hatchet.

Yet Talbot was admitting to participation in the murder, and that in itself was a hanging offence. The question remained: Why? Talbot supplied the answer without hesitation. Annie had double-crossed him.

The two Guards were aware of the incident of the previous year, when the suspect had gone to the Walshe house with a gun – and assaulted Annie. She'd received compensation and Talbot had gone to jail. Kenny had thought at the time that the circumstances surrounding the case were odd. That Talbot had threatened Walshe with a gun was credible: he had a reputation in the district for rowdy behaviour, especially when drink was involved, and was known to quarrel often with Walshe. But there'd been no good reason for the assault on Annie. Now Talbot supplied clarification.

'Didn't she get £20 over the last case,' he said. 'And she divided it with me. "Come over Friday night," she told me, and we'll kill Ned." She said she'd get compensation out of his death and she'd give half to me. She said that she'd sell the house and the two of us would go away together. She wanted to be rid of the Walshes.'

It was beginning to make sense. The assault on Annie had been a sham, possibly prearranged. The pair had reckoned they could fool the authorities again, this time for greater reward. Now Annie was growing greedy: she was prepared to let her nephew go to the gallows for her husband's murder. She'd be rid of all the Walshes and have enough money to enable her to settle elsewhere.

'Tell us about the murder itself,' Kenny urged.

'I called at the Walshe house on the following night at ten o'clock,' said Talbot. 'The door was open and Annie and her husband were carrying a big stick into the kitchen. The stick fell against the door. Annie said that her arm was hurt and she asked me to help them.

'We stood talking by the kitchen fire for a couple of hours, and then Annie asked Ned to go out for another stick to keep the fire red. When he was going out she picked up a hatchet and put it under her apron. Presently Ned came back with a stick and sat down in front of the fire. Annie immediately lowered the light and brought the hatchet down on his head, and he fell right across the fire, kicking.'

'What did you do then?'

'She told me to hold his hands. I held them. She drew a second blow at him and he didn't stir any more. She brought the light into the bedroom and asked me to stay with her until morning. She said she'd go to the Guards when I was gone, and that she'd get the money out of his death and give me half of it, and we'd go away. She said she'd sell the cottage. I stopped there until half past six in the morning in the bed with her. I went away then home.

She gave me a ring and a Sacred Heart badge when I was going away. She told me not to let the Guards see me until she would get the money.'

Guard Kenny was gobsmacked. In a few sentences Talbot had confessed not only to complicity in murder but also to having an affair with his aunt. The pair had shared a bed while the corpse of Annie's husband was lying beside the fire in the adjoining room. Kenny would never know how long they'd been conducting the illicit relationship. Nor did he want to know. The burning issue was murder. No doubt the other unsavoury facts would come out at the trial. . . .

The love affair did, however, go a long way to explain both the present events and those of the previous year. It was entirely possible that Edward Walshe had found out about it, hence the visit and its resulting violence, for which Talbot had been sent to prison. If that were true then Talbot was lying about what had happened on the night of the murder. If Walshe and he were love-rivals then the dead man would certainly not have allowed him near his home. To Kenny it seemed more plausible that Annie's story was closer to the truth: Talbot had entered the house as an intruder.

The Guards searched the suspect and found on his person the items he'd spoken about: the religious medal and the ring. At least that part was true. They arrested him.

Down at the station in Limerick the police brought Annie and her nephew face to face. She was confronted with her nephew's statement, accusing her of being the principal perpetrator. She grew very angry – and changed her story once again.

At twelve o'clock, she said, when her husband and she were in bed, Talbot knocked on the door. She called out: 'No admission after hours!' Talbot forced the door and entered the kitchen, drunk. The three went and sat by the fire; the men had a row and Talbot struck Walshe with his fist. He ordered her to lower the lamp. She refused and he did so instead. Then he shot her husband in the head. He remained in the house till morning, keeping her prisoner and restraining her by a hand around her throat.

As the days went by it became increasingly difficult to decide who was lying: Annie Walshe or her nephew. Perhaps both. The case came to the County Courthouse in Limerick on 17 November, and the jurors heard the three conflicting stories – with further embellishments.

The first was that related by Annie: that a mystery gunman had shot her husband in their home. But Talbot's account made a nonsense this. At least his version of events chimed with Dr Hederman's conclusion: Edward Walshe hadn't been shot but bludgeoned to death.

Talbot, she said, was lying. He'd come to her home unexpectedly on the Friday night and forced in the door. He'd entered the kitchen and taken a revolver from his pocket. When her husband tried to disarm him Talbot knocked him to the floor and shot him through the head.

Then he turned on Annie. He grabbed her by the throat and forced her down on the floor. He threatened to kill her as well if she went to the police.

No verdict could be brought in and the case was returned for trial, again in Limerick, at the Court of Jurisdiction, and again the jury failed to reach a verdict. The case went before the Central Criminal Court, in Green Street, Dublin.

Mr Justice Hanna heard the conflicting evidence and ordered that both prisoners be tried separately. Talbot was first: he was tried on Thursday, 9 July 1925, and found guilty of murder. Two days later Annie appeared before Hanna. The verdict was the same.

'I did not kill my husband!' Annie protested against all the evidence to the contrary. The gardaí – notably Guard Kenny – had done their jobs well and the judge commended them on their high standard of procedure and their ability. Kenny's testimony had dispelled all reasonable doubt that Annie and her nephew had planned and carried out her husband's murder.

In so many of the cases recounted in these pages a jury bringing in a verdict of guilty recommended clemency for a female prisoner. This time there was no such plea. As far as the jurors were concerned, Annie Walshe deserved to be put to death. It was her treachery that doomed her. Had she not turned on Talbot in an attempt to gain maximum profit from an innocent man's death, then leniency would no doubt have been shown. By her greed and duplicity she'd lost all hope of compassion from the jury.

Hanna donned the black cap and pronounced sentence. He was making history. The last woman to hang in Ireland was Mary Daly, convicted jointly with her lover for the killing of her husband. She was executed in 1903.

It was a double hanging in Mountjoy Prison on Wednesday, 5 August 1925. As usual Pierpoint, the State Executioner, veteran of so many hangings, carried out Mr Justice Hanna's orders.

Pierpoint knew his job. Dr Louis Byrne conducted an inquest on the corpses of Annie and her lover, and stated that death in both cases had been instantaneous. Annie and her lover were buried within the prison walls.

Hannah O'Leary and
the Fields of Horror

In the late afternoon of 7 March 1924 a boy of ten was crossing a field in Kilkerrin, a townland about four miles from Clonakilty, County Cork. He noticed a potato sack hidden under a furze bush and stopped to examine it. He got the fright of his life. It contained a human head, hideously battered.

The police were notified of the gruesome find and two Guards hurried to the scene. The light was fading when they arrived and one of them took the lamp from his bicycle. The other summoned the owner of the field: Cornelius O'Leary, known to all as Con. The policemen had recognized the head but wished to be certain. O'Leary stared calmly at it, then said after a moment: 'Yes, that's Pat.' The head was that of his brother.

Thus began a search of the field, and others in the vicinity. Piece by horrible piece, the body of Pat O'Leary was reassembled. The pieces lay scattered over a radius of 600 yards from the O'Leary farmhouse; some were discovered on their land, others on neighbouring properties. Bizarrely, the person or persons who'd slain O'Leary and dismembered his body had gone to no lengths at all to truly conceal the parts. Nothing was buried.

An arm was found that same evening in a second sack, lying among some furze, just thirty-seven yards from the house.

The right leg lay in plain view in a gorse field 110 yards from the house; the other was discovered nine yards farther on. The police found part of the torso on the property of a neighbour, in a dilapidated hut known as Deasy's Ruins; another lay forty-four yards from the O'Leary house, in a field owned by the Walsh family. These body parts were found the following day.

In the meantime the Guards had collected the head and right arm, and brought them to a nearby village. In a room behind a public house Con's sisters Hannah and Mary Anne were invited to identify the head. They too appeared unmoved by the awful sight. Hannah merely glanced at it, then looked away.

Superintendent Mark Troy, who'd taken charge of the investigation, sent Mary Anne out of the room. He then coaxed Hannah into making a more thorough examination.

'Look at the temples,' he said. 'There's no hair growing there. Wasn't that the case with your brother Pat?'

Hannah conceded that this was indeed so, yet still couldn't say for certain that the severed head had once sat on her brother's neck. Her face was without expression when she said this; Troy couldn't believe that Hannah and her sister showed so little emotion when confronted with the sight of their brother's mutilated remains. It wasn't natural.

He turned the head so that Hannah could see it face on.

'Now,' he said, 'is this Pat?'

Hannah couldn't bring herself to look straight into her

dead brother's eyes. She peered at them out of the corner
of her own.

'No,' she said at last. 'Pat was not so thin in the poll.'

Looks of disbelief were exchanged in the room. Troy
recalled Mary Anne. She identified the head as Pat's. He
turned again to Hannah. She studied it more closely, yet
again denied it was her brother's. Troy asked her a third
time.

'I'm beginning to think it is him,' she said after a time.
After an even longer time she nodded. 'Yes, 'tis Pat sure
enough.'

Pat O'Leary had been missing for ten days prior to the
discovery of his scattered remains. At an inquest held
on 8 March, the day after the finding of the head, his
brother Con made his deposition. He sketched the family
background.

The father, Patrick O'Leary, died in 1921, leaving behind property worth £1,100 – a substantial sum in those
days. He left all to his widow Hannah. On her death the
property would go to Pat, the elder son. Both Con and
Hannah junior would have right of residence for life;
Mary Anne, the younger daughter, was to receive a lump
sum of £350 on her mother's death.

In the event of Pat's death the farm would be divided
among the survivors. It is likely that Con would have got
the lion's share. Whether Hannah and Mary Anne would
have been better off financially is not known. What is
known is that all three would benefit *emotionally* from
Pat's death.

His siblings disliked him intensely, for he was a brutal
man who made no bones about who was master of the
O'Leary property. Con slept at home but didn't work the

farm: he was employed by a farmer named William Travers. This arrangement was a bone of contention for Pat. Three times he'd visited Con's employer, demanding that his brother leave the job and come to help work the family farm – without a wage. Farmer Travers had taken exception to these intrusions and given Con notice to quit.

Mary Anne shunned the O'Leary farm, preferring to live elsewhere. She worked for a neighbour, who gave her food and lodgings together with a small wage. Hannah had little choice but to stay and skivvy for her overbearing elder brother. Nothing is known of Mrs O'Leary's relationship with Pat, yet it cannot have been amicable, as the investigation was to show.

At the inquest Con stated that he'd last seen his brother alive a little before ten o'clock on Monday, 25 February, when Pat had retired for the night. For some reason, left unexplained, Pat slept in the loft of an outhouse, in a bed between a store of potatoes and feed for the livestock. He had, Con stated, left the house before dawn on the Tuesday but Con hadn't heard him either enter or exit the house, he being fast asleep in his bedroom beside the kitchen. Hannah had prepared breakfast and was therefore the last person to see Pat that day. Hannah had informed Con that Pat had departed for the fair in Bandon with the intention of selling a colt.

The difficulty was that the colt was still in its stable; Con had watered and fed it in the days following his brother's disappearance.

Did Con not think it odd, Superintendent Troy wished to know, when Pat didn't return from the fair?

Evidently not.

'No,' Con stated. 'I made no search for my brother since the twenty-seventh of February.'

'Did you ask any person if they'd seen him?'

'I did not. I thought he'd turn up any minute. I didn't think he'd go away and leave the place after him. I thought he was gone away to work somewhere – to Cork or England or somewhere else.'

'What about your mother and sisters?' Troy asked. 'Were they not also wondering why Patrick hadn't returned?'

'They were. They discussed it with me.'

'And did ye arrive at any conclusion?'

'We did not.'

It was all too implausible. Why would Pat suddenly up and leave behind a valuable property that was to be his upon his mother's death? And why, when Pat was missing for such a long time, did the family not alert the authorities?

It was obvious to Superintendent Troy that whoever killed Pat lived at the O'Leary home. He thought it highly unlikely that an outsider had done Pat to death, dismembered his body and left the pieces lying half-hidden so close to the house. Moreover Con's deposition contradicted itself in places: little things, but they pointed to dishonesty. Furthermore there was a possible motive: Pat O'Leary's overbearingness.

But which of the O'Learys was the murderer? Mary Anne was strong enough; so was Hannah. Con could have battered his brother to death with his bare hands. The mother had allowed ten days to elapse without going to the authorities. Troy arrested all four O'Learys on 14 March.

All were guilty in his eyes. The neighbours had told him about the wake. . . .

The wake is a tradition that still lives on in rural Ireland, though it isn't as common as it once was. In 1924 it was part and parcel of the rites of death and it would have been considered unnatural if the O'Leary family had not 'waked' their dead brother and son.

As it was, Mrs O'Leary, Con, Hannah and Mary Anne showed themselves to be so unnatural in their grief that those friends and neighbours present at the wake were appalled. Pat's remains were displayed in a coffin without a lid.

It is hard to imagine a more gruesome tableau than the one that greeted the visitors who entered the O'Leary home that night, 9 March, two days after the head had been found in the field. The kitchen was the focus of the wake. There was whiskey and porter in good quantities, tea for the teetotallers, sandwiches and cake. In keeping with tradition the coffin was propped against a wall, the corpse in plain view. At least somebody had gone to the trouble of putting some clothing on Pat's remains. Yet it was impossible to disguise the fact that the head had been crudely severed from the neck, that the body resembled a Frankenstein monster – and one moreover that was incomplete; not all the body parts had been recovered. It was too much for one guest, and he said so when he'd plucked up sufficient Dutch courage.

'I must certainly say, Con,' he complained, ''tis a terrible state of affairs to see your brother cut up in pieces and you not a bit worried over it. I must also say, Con, that suspicions are strongly against you and 'tis up to you to find the perpetrator and free yourself.'

Another guest agreed, and rounded on Con's mother.

''Tis a shame, Mrs O'Leary,' she said, 'to see your son in such a state and 'tis easily known who done it.'

Con felt cornered. 'I'm innocent!' he protested.

His mother and sisters said nothing – and their silence was the most searing indictment of all. The guests at the wake couldn't believe their callousness. And it *was* easily known 'who done it'.

For crass stupidity the O'Leary family were hard to beat; the investigators could not but conclude that the family hailed from the paddling end of the gene pool. Every single clue pointed to their guilt, and they'd done the barest minimum to cover their tracks. The sane mind must surely boggle at their botched disposal of Pat's dismembered corpse – so careless was this that while the Guards were searching for body parts, the O'Learys' dog appeared carrying a severed arm in its mouth. A piece of ticking – sackcloth used for bedding – was found in the grass not seventy yards from the farmhouse. It was blood-stained and matched another piece found under Con's bed.

By the same token the gardaí were bemused by the sheer incompetence of the murderers' attempts to conceal the scene of the crime. Somebody had changed the bedclothes and mattress of Pat's bed in the loft, yet the investigators found copious bloodstains – some under the bed, others even bespattering the pile of potatoes nearby. The headboard of the bed had been wiped clean – though an examination of holes and cracks in the wood revealed more dried blood. There was even blood on the ceiling, a testimony to the violence by which Pat had met his end. It was obvious that the horrific act of butchery had taken place here.

There were some old clothes lying on the bed. Troy asked Con who owned them and was told they belonged to Pat. And his brother's best clothes? Con said he'd been wearing them when going to the fair.

The gardaí searched the loft and found the remains of a bloodstained mattress. Again, the murderer had made little effort to conceal it. The mattress matched pieces found in neighbouring fields and under Con's bed.

The jagged edges of the wounds to Pat's neck and severed limbs indicated that the instrument of butchery must have been fairly blunt, therefore ruling out a razor or sharp knife. A hatchet would have done the job; the Guards found one but it bore no trace of blood. The coroner concluded that Pat had died in his sleep; there were no marks on the body which would indicate a struggle. His killer had pounded the head almost to a pulp, possibly with a hammer, before dismembering the body.

The police continued to search the area around the farmhouse. Con went with Troy to an overgrown garden and they found a pair of trousers in the undergrowth; another officer uncovered a matching jacket in an adjacent field. Con declared the items to be his brother's best suit – the one Pat was supposed to have been wearing on the morning of his disappearance.

Troy believed that the whole family had colluded in the slaying yet couldn't be certain. Hannah and Mary Anne provided evidence of a sort. One of the Guards began to search a field at the back of the house. He paused on noticing that the sisters were following his movements with great interest. He searched even more diligently and, sure enough, came upon a severed leg.

A date was set for the trial of all four O'Learys. What Troy and the other investigators didn't know, however, was that Mary Anne had been suffering from bowel cancer for a number of years. At the time of her arrest it was in its final stage; she died in prison on 3 May.

The prosecution had no case against Mrs O'Leary. She pleaded innocent to murder or conspiracy to murder. While that may have been so, it is difficult to see how the murder could have been kept from her, and why she didn't query her elder son's disappearance. But she was seventy-five and the case against her was dropped.

That left Hannah and Con to share the guilt equally. Wisely their defence counsel, Joseph McCarthy, refused to allow either of them into the box; Con's poor performance at the inquest had shown him to be a very unreliable witness. Instead McCarthy attempted to place the blame on Mary Anne. The judge was having none of it.

'Mr McCarthy,' he said, 'you are not entitled to make the case to the jury that Mary Anne did it. You have given no evidence whatever as regards that.'

'You seem to preclude me, m'lud,' McCarthy said, 'from making any observations to show that neither of the prisoners participated in this crime.'

To which the judge responded: 'When you are not producing either of the prisoners to give evidence you cannot make the case or the suggestion that Mary Anne did it. If you can point out to the jury any portion of evidence which shows Mary Anne may have done it, you are entitled to.'

McCarthy could not, though he might easily have shown that Mary Anne was equally implicated. Had she not watched with Hannah as the Guard combed the field where Pat's missing leg was found?

The jury, however, could not fail to find Hannah and Con guilty and having retired for an hour they did so. For some reason they recommended clemency for Hannah; perhaps they felt that of the two Con was more capable of the revolting crime. The judge took note but wasn't swayed: he sentenced both to death.

The verdict was appealed, partly on the grounds that the trial judge hadn't allowed for the possibility that Mary Anne had committed – or helped to commit – the murder. Michael Comyn, counsel for Con and Hannah, pointed out that the trial hadn't brought out 'one scintilla of evidence of common purpose, of concert to commit murder'; therefore the admissions of one prisoner couldn't be used as evidence against the other.

Furthermore, Comyn said, Pat had not been killed in his sleep, that he might have lived for several days after being attacked, and that his attacker might have been a stranger.

But the sheer brutality involved in the murder went against the O'Learys. The appeal judge learned the reason why Pat's remains had been preserved for so long. The local doctor told him that the weather was cold and the body, having been disembowelled, would remain fresh longer than usual.

'And where were the remains kept?' the judge asked.

'They were kept for a week in the house,' the doctor said, 'like flitches of bacon.'

'Did the family live there with the dismembered remains?' asked the incredulous judge.

'I believe so.'

'If that is true,' said his lordship, looking fixedly at the prisoners, 'then they must be the most hideous of human beings.'

The appeal failed.

Con was hanged in Mountjoy Prison on 28 July 1925. The murder and the horrific 'disposal' of the body parts were so shocking that one of the O'Learys' neighbours had been rendered temporarily insane when confronted with the facts. Seconds before his death Con was to elicit disgust in somebody else: one of the warders officiating at the execution fainted and had to receive medical attention.

Hannah fared better than her brother. She was granted a reprieve three days before her execution date and her sentence commuted to life imprisonment. She was released from Mountjoy in 1942 on condition that she enter the convent where she spent the rest of her days.

Unlike her brother Pat she died peacefully in her bed, in 1967.

Annabella Hunter, the Lodger with the Large Suitcase

Drew Street once lay in the Grosvenor Road area of Belfast. It was a narrow street of two-storey, red-brick houses in the shadow of the Royal Victoria Hospital. The houses were demolished soon after World War II, and part of the new maternity wing of the hospital covers the original site of 27 Drew Street. This is, as the following story will show, a grisly coincidence.

Mary Cheadle had owned the house from the 1880s. She was a widow, living alone and, in order to supplement her modest pension, she took lodgers. She was seventy-five when in 1925 a young woman knocked on her door requesting a room to rent. By Mrs Cheadle's account she was friendly, if somewhat introvert; she was dressed soberly and clearly not a woman of means.

Annabella Hamilton was twenty-five at the time. She hailed from Randalstown, County Antrim, and was the second daughter of a God-fearing Presbyterian shopkeeper. On learning of her intention of going to Belfast to work as an assistant in a milliner's shop, her parents had given her a Bible as well as other religious tracts and hymnals, in order that their daughter's mind should remain pure amid the many temptations of the city.

To Mrs Cheadle it would have appeared that the quiet-spoken young woman had followed her parents' good counsel to the letter; she seemed a picture of respectability. Annabella was, then, an unremarkable lodger. There was little about her that was likely to draw attention, with the exception, perhaps, of a large suitcase. The case wasn't locked – the landlady could testify to that fact. Annabella told her, unprompted, that it contained books and clothing.

Mrs Cheadle gave her young lodger a back bedroom, which was to become Annabella's home for the next six years. She kept very much to herself during those years and the landlady knew little of her business. It came as a surprise, therefore, when her lodger told her she was to be married. Annabella had never entertained guests in the house and as far as Mrs Cheadle knew had never kept male company.

John Hunter was the husband-to-be. He was a Belfast-man and a cabinet-maker by trade. The pair married on 4 July 1931 and, with Mrs Cheadle's blessing, settled into 27 Drew Street. She rented the newly-weds a bigger room at the front of the house.

Annabella's large suitcase remained under the bed in her old room.

Five months later, on 1 December, the couple left to set up a home of their own in Baltic Street, near the Belfast Royal Academy. What struck the landlady at the time was that Annabella had moved out taking with her very few belongings. She left behind all her shoes, several hats, books, and some odds and ends. Mrs Cheadle recalled the suitcase Annabella had with her the first day but assumed that her lodger had disposed of it sometime during the intervening six years. She thought no more about it.

On 3 January 1932, Mrs Cheadle was visited by her sister, Ellie Burns. Ellie was accompanied by her son Trevor and daughter Margaret.

As soon as the trio entered the house they were aware of a very heavy and disagreeable odour that seemed to come from upstairs. Mrs Cheadle told them she noticed nothing. This might have been due to a deterioration in the elderly lady's faculties; equally, she might have lived with the smell so long as to be no longer conscious of it – as a perfume is smelled more strongly by others than by its wearer.

In any event Margaret Burns climbed the stairs to investigate, and soon discovered the source of the noisome odour: it emanated from a locked suitcase under the bed in one of the back rooms. She lifted it out and carried it down into the backyard. Her brother Trevor forced the lock.

The case contained two copies of the Bible and a number of other books. On the flyleaf of one was written the name 'Mrs J Hunter'. Trevor found items of clothing, all packed tightly. There were four small objects wrapped in separate pieces of cloth and these he removed. To his horror he saw they were small corpses, all in an advanced state of decomposition. Examination would reveal that the oldest had been in the suitcase for about twelve years.

News of the find spread quickly through the district and soon the house in Drew Street was the talk of Belfast. The police were called in and they interviewed Mrs Cheadle. Yes, she knew who the suitcase belonged to but Annabella had left no forwarding address. Nevertheless the police located her at the house in Baltic Street. She was very ill with a bad attack of influenza.

They arrested her on the charge that she, 'at Belfast at

various times within the last twelve years, having been delivered of four children, did by secret disposition of the dead bodies of such children endeavour to conceal the birth thereof.' Annabella was remanded and, because of her illness, brought to the Union Infirmary.

It was agreed that an inquest should be held. The Belfast coroner, Dr James Graham, took the stand on 12 January and told the magistrate of his findings.

The post-mortem identified the bodies as being those of newly born infants, yet Graham could not say whether they'd been delivered alive or stillborn. Nor had he been able to form an opinion as to the cause of death in each case.

The appearance of the corpses told him that they'd 'existed, in a dead state, for several years after birth'. So decomposed were three of the bodies that Graham was unable to identify their gender; he was certain, however, that the fourth was male.

The doctor was then requested to submit his findings in detail. Graham stated that the first body was completely mummified. It was some nineteen inches long – about the normal length of a newborn child – and there was no indication of a premature birth. The stomach, internal organs and brain, he said, had completely disappeared during the process of mummification. When asked if he'd found evidence of foul play, Graham replied that there was no sign of fracturing to the skull, constriction of the neck or wounds to the rest of the body.

The second corpse was that of another newborn child, again some nineteen inches long and completely mummified. The umbilical cord appeared to have been severed by a sharp instrument. As was the case with the first body, stomach, internal organs and brain had disappeared.

Graham had again concluded there was no indication of death by violent means. This was true also of the third body. It was likewise mummified and the umbilical cord severed by a sharp instrument. The doctor had found an inch-long growth of hair on the head, and the nails on the fingers and toes were fully developed.

The remaining corpse was definitely that of a male child, mummified and about eighteen inches long. Parts of the face were missing. The stomach had disappeared but there were remains of the lungs. Yet again, Graham found no signs of physical abuse.

The first body was the latest, the doctor declared, and suggested it had been in the suitcase for fewer than two years. Graham told the inquest board he believed that all four infants had been born alive, though he couldn't state this with certainty.

The board then called the first witness, Mrs Cheadle, who gave a brief account of Annabella Hunter's stay at her home. She told the assembly that the suitcase belonged to Annabella. No, she had never seen it open.

The inquest board next called Mrs Cheadle's sister, Ellie Burns, followed by her daughter Margaret, her son Trevor, and Detective Constable Evans, the police officer who'd examined the contents of the case.

Evans stated that, in addition to the bodies, there were a number of books. One bore the name 'Anne Hamilton' on the flyleaf, another 'Mrs J Hunter'.

This last was an important piece of evidence. Annabella Hamilton had become Mrs John Hunter on 4 July 1931, six months before the bodies were found.

The suitcase was clearly hers, and so it was that on 22 February 1932 she appeared before Lord Justice Best, charged with concealing the births of four children.

Murder can hide behind any number of euphemisms but 'concealment of birth' or 'secret disposition' must rank among the more callous. If we are to believe the court records of Ireland – north and south – then giving birth to a stillborn baby was the norm rather than the exception where single mothers were concerned. Living as we do in relatively enlightened times, when the rights of the unborn child are defended with as much passion as the rights of the neonate, we may find it hard to accept that up until comparatively recently the death of an infant born outside wedlock sometimes passed largely unnoticed. In fact its death was often welcomed – or treated as 'God's will'.

Had Annabella Hunter's suitcase been large enough to contain the corpses of four adults, we can be sure she'd have been before the court on four charges of murder. As it was, there were 'only' the corpses of four infants.

Did anybody query how the babies had met their end? Or if they were dead when placed in the suitcase? Surprisingly enough it was Annabella's own defence counsel who raised the matter. He submitted to the judge that in order that the Crown 'might sustain the indictment they must prove secret disposition of the dead body of a child'.

He was opening a can of worms, and Lord Justice Best warned him of this. But not before Campbell made the following extraordinary statement.

'It would be within my rights', he said, 'to say that at the time of the secret disposition the children were not dead at all and are therefore outside this indictment.'

In other words: If my client stuffed the babies into the suitcase *alive* then she cannot be tried for unlawfully disposing of four *dead* children.

'If you get off on that ground,' the judge cautioned,

'then your client will find herself in a much more perilous position.'

Campbell must have realized at this point that he'd put his foot in it – and risked putting Annabella's neck in a noose. He quickly back-pedalled.

'I did not urge that, m'lud,' he said, 'but stated it for the purpose of argument.'

Annabella had appeared in court holding yet another child, about six weeks' old. She had therefore given birth to at least five children. What was different about her latest child was the fact that it had been born within marriage. Were the four illegitimate children in the suitcase stillborn – and the legitimate child the only one to survive birth? This surely would be stretching coincidence too far. Yet in the course of the trial nobody saw fit to comment on this. While Annabella attended the trial, her infant was cared for by a woman officer of the Salvation Army.

In her defence Campbell told the court there was no evidence that his client had given birth to the four children, or that the defendant had placed the bodies in the suitcase. Annabella, he maintained, knew nothing about them.

The suitcase was exhibited in the court and remained in view throughout the trial. There was hardly a man or woman present who could keep their eyes from it.

The Crown prosecutor, William McGonigle, called Mrs Cheadle as the first witness. She identified the suitcase as belonging to Annabella. People visiting the house, she said, had sometimes complained of a bad smell.

'Did you detect this bad smell yourself?' McGonigle asked.

'Never.'

'Did you ever see the case open?'

'Never.'

The landlady then recounted how her nephew Trevor had forced the case open and discovered its grisly contents. He'd called the police.

It was Campbell's turn to cross-examine. He asked Mrs Cheadle who else besides Annabella had access to the room.

'Anyone could go in there,' Mrs Cheadle replied. 'Her bedroom was never locked.'

'Did the suitcase always occupy the same place?'

'Yes.'

The onus was therefore on the prosecution to prove that Annabella had placed the corpses in the case. There was no evidence she'd ever handled it.

'Except', Lord Justice Best reminded him, 'that when she came to the house she had the case and it was under her control all that time.'

Campbell insisted there was open access to the room; the judge replied that that was not the evidence. He called Annabella to the witness box and she declared her innocence.

McGonigle questioned her about the smell in the house – and particularly in the bedroom she'd occupied.

'Were you ever annoyed by a bad smell when you were there?' he asked.

'No.'

'Have you a good sense of smell?' the judge wished to know.

She replied she had.

'Did you ever receive complaints about a bad smell?'

'No one ever mentioned one while I was there.'

She denied again that the children in the suitcase were

hers and had no idea whose they were.

'Did you ever open the case during all the time to see the things that were yours?' McGonigle asked.

'No,' said Annabella. 'I had not any call for it.'

'May I take it that you never opened the case while it was in Mrs Cheadle's?'

'Oh, no. I opened it nine months ago, when I was putting embroidery in it.'

'Was there any body of an infant in it then?'

'No.'

'And you locked it then?'

'Yes.'

'And the only one living in the house with you was Mrs Cheadle?'

'Yes.'

'You don't suggest', McGonigle said, 'that Mrs Cheadle put the bodies in the suitcase?'

'I do not.'

'Do you know of anyone who may have done it?'

'No.'

The infamous suitcase had lain unopened in the courtroom during the course of the trial. The final witness called was Detective Constable Evans, the arresting officer. Having heard how he'd open the suitcase the judge asked him to do so again. Evans hesitated.

'It would cause a very bad smell,' he protested.

'We can't help the smell,' Best said. 'We've had worse smells in this court,' he added, thereby eliciting the first and only laughter to be heard during the grim proceedings.

Evans then went on to describe how the tiny corpses had been wrapped in items of ladies' clothing, paper and sacking. People in the public gallery listened in silence.

The jury found Annabella guilty of concealment of birth and she was returned a fortnight later to receive her sentence. Campbell had engaged another barrister, Peter Marrinan, to defend his client. No doubt he felt her case was hopeless but was willing to allow another to salvage what could yet be salvaged.

Marrinan tried to appeal to Best's sense of decency. He reminded the judge that Annabella came from a good Christian home and that she herself was a very religious person. Unfortunately, finding herself removed from the good influence of her parents, she'd encountered temptation in Belfast and fallen in love with a dishonest man. She'd given birth to four of his children before he'd deserted her. Annabella, Marrinan pleaded, was a victim, not a criminal.

'Someone has shown her no mercy,' he concluded, 'and she now throws herself upon your lordship's mercy.'

It was a fine speech and Best was moved by it. He did, however, point out that Annabella had wasted two days of the court's time by denying her guilt; now that the trial was over and sentence was about to be passed, she was finally admitting to having tried to conceal the births of four children by enclosing their bodies in a locked suitcase. Annabella might be a God-fearing woman but was as guilty as sin. He turned to the woman in the dock.

'You were defended with great ability,' he said to her, 'but notwithstanding the defence the jury found you guilty of the charge. If this was an isolated case I might be inclined to pass it over, but it cannot go forth from this court that conduct of this kind in reference to little children brought into the world can be tolerated.'

Lord Justice Best went on to say that he was taking

into consideration the fact that Annabella was now married and rearing a small child. Nevertheless the sentence he was imposing was a custodial one – in compliance with the law. He sent her down for nine months.

If this was an isolated case . . . Before leaving the case of Annabella Hunter née Hamilton we might pause to consider the judge's words – and those words he left unsaid. She'd given birth not to one but to four illegitimate children, and disposed of them all. Conduct of this nature certainly couldn't be tolerated.

But before we condemn her out of hand it may also be worth considering Annabella's circumstances. Twelve years or more before the trial she'd found herself pregnant by a man she thought she loved. She could not keep his child and had to dispose of it. (Let us give Annabella the benefit of the doubt and assume it was stillborn or had died soon after birth.) She had to get rid of the little corpse. How? She could hardly throw it into the Lagan like a sackful of unwanted kittens. And what would Mrs Cheadle have thought had she chanced upon Annabella burying the body in the back garden of 27 Drew Street in the dead of night? Annabella was too 'respectable' for such actions.

She could, like Jane Lawther, have persuaded a gravedigger to bury the child in consecrated ground and paid him with money and several glasses of whiskey for his pains. Yet this too is an unlikely scenario. I doubt if Annabella would have had the gumption to organize it, much less carry it out.

And so, in sheer desperation, she chose to swaddle the dead baby in old clothes and brown paper, and stuff it into her suitcase. No one need ever know; she didn't even have to venture out of doors, or even out of her own room. Probably the notion that decomposing flesh gives off a nauseating odour had never occurred to her.

But she got pregnant again – and repeated the ghastly operation. And yet again. Four times in all. She did it to protect not only her own family name but also that of the man who made her pregnant and subsequently deserted her.

Annabella never spoke again about the four dead children: at least not to anyone in Crumlin Road jail or to those who'd defended her. On her release from prison on 19 December 1932 she and her husband left for London with their little son, taking the secrets of the suitcase with them.

Mary Cole, the Vengeful Teenager from County Laois

Michael and Anastasia Flynn loved children: their own and those whom they taught at the local primary school in Camross, a little village close to Rathdowney, County Laois. When Mrs Flynn was pregnant with her third child in August 1926 the couple decided to employ a second domestic servant; this arrangement would leave them both free to pursue their careers, in the knowledge that their children were being looked after.

Mary Cole, a thirteen-year-old, seemed suitable. The Flynns had taught her at the primary school before her parents moved to Mountrath, near Portlaoise. At the interview she expressed a keen desire to work and was moreover accustomed to living on a farm; she could perform household tasks, take care of the children and look after the livestock. Best of all she displayed a great fondness for children. All appeared in order and Mary moved into the Flynn home in September.

Yet as the weeks went by a different Mary Cole began to emerge. The Flynns had to caution her about her language. It wasn't overly coarse, yet the swear words sat uneasily in the mouth of a young girl. Worse, the Flynns' eldest child, five-year-old Maureen, had begun to pick up undesirable words. Mrs Flynn spoke to Mary about it; Mary promised to mend her ways.

The real trouble started early in 1927 when Mary had turned fourteen. Michael Flynn overheard some of the senior boys in his school talking and laughing among themselves. He heard the name Mary Cole mentioned a couple of times. Flynn took one boy aside and demanded to know what was being said. The youngster's words shocked him. He learned that Mary was in the habit of 'entertaining' a group of boys from the district. At night, while the Flynns slept, the boys would come round to Mary's window and engage her in conversation. It was also rumoured that one of the boys had actually entered the girl's bedroom.

Flynn told his wife of his suspicions and she confronted Mary. The girl denied everything; the boys were lying. Mrs Flynn was unconvinced; she wanted the truth. She called on Father Walshe, the parish priest, and asked him to come and have a word with Mary. Walshe had a fearsome reputation; if there was wrongdoing and scandal then the priest would get to the bottom of it. He rounded up the two ringleaders from the school and frogmarched them to the Flynns' house.

Mary stood her ground; she'd done nothing wrong, she told the priest. He didn't believe her, took Mrs Flynn aside and urged her to speak sternly to the girl. Mrs Flynn did, and elicited a startling confession from Mary: not only was it true that the boys made nocturnal calls on her but Mary had actually left the house after nightfall and spent the night with one of them.

Mrs Flynn struggled to come to terms with this confession. Mary Cole was only fourteen, after all, and her behaviour was totally unacceptable in County Laois in 1927. Such a scandal would surely reflect badly on the Flynns and their important position within the community. Her first thought was to dismiss Mary and she spoke to Father Walshe about it. The priest may have had a fearsome reputation but he was also a man of Christian virtues; he disagreed with Mrs Flynn's decision.

'The poor Magdalen,' he said of Mary. 'Keep her and be a mother to her.'

The good man wasn't to know it was the worst advice he could have given. Mrs Flynn had already been something of a mother to Mary. She was generous to a fault and had even made the girl a present of a highly fashionable navy outfit and a sweater. On consideration, Mrs Flynn now believed that the clothes might have given Mary ideas beyond her age; they made her look older. She believed the outfit had made Mary 'giddy'.

She decided to have a word with the girl's mother. Mrs Cole was horrified to hear about her daughter's behaviour and agreed with Mrs Flynn that she should take back the clothes. Mrs Flynn, she said, was 'spoiling' Mary. A little humiliation might be good for her.

But no one – not even her own mother – could have guessed the depth of resentment Mary Cole felt. Her love life was her own business, she believed, and nobody – not her mother, not her employer, not the parish priest – had a right to interfere in it. She vowed to teach Mrs Flynn a lesson. . . .

It was 27 July 1927 and little Philomena Flynn would be two in September. School was finished for the summer; Mrs Flynn had more time to devote to her home. Her husband was busy once more on the land, catching up on work that needed to be done. Today he'd left for Rath-downey, where the local agricultural show was held.

Mrs Flynn had had a long day. She'd forgotten how demanding the children could be. The eldest, Maureen, was nearly seven; the youngest, Michael, was not yet a year old. Mrs Flynn had given the family an early dinner and gone upstairs to lie down; she intended having a nap until six o'clock, when the cow was due to be milked. The Flynns were in the habit of having this done in a byre next to the house; it meant not having to carry a heavy pail from the field.

Mrs Flynn heard the angelus bell ringing, said her prayers and came down into the kitchen. Kate Tobin, the other servant, and Mary Cole were there, the latter feeding the infant Michael from a bottle. Mrs Flynn told her it was time to fetch the cow for milking; this was Mary's task. Since the incident with the boys and the priest the girl had gone about her duties sullenly and had to be reminded about the most elementary things.

Mary, bad-humoured as ever, told Mrs Flynn that the calf needed food and there was none left. She got money to buy some and set off for Phelan's shop – a short distance down the road.

Mary returned some minutes later. Michael was in his crib, six-year-old Maureen was playing in the kitchen – but there was no sign of Philomena. Mrs Flynn asked Mary if she'd seen the toddler.

'No,' was the reply. 'Perhaps she's upstairs. She was there a few minutes ago.'

Mrs Flynn checked the children's room; Philomena was nowhere to be found. She grew extremely concerned; the child was much too young to go off on her own; the servant girls had strict instructions not to let any of the children out of their sight.

Mrs Flynn set off through the fields surrounding the house, calling out Philomena's name as she went. No sign. She went farther afield, almost as far as the river Nore. Still no sign of her little girl. On the way back to the house the worried mother met Mary Cole and Kate Tobin; both girls joined in the search.

A neighbour, John Gorman, came on the scene and Mrs Flynn told him about the disappearance. He immediately offered to help and headed in the direction of the river. Here he came upon Mary, who looked upset.

'It would be an awful thing', she said, 'if Philomena was drowned.'

Mary proved to be remarkably prescient, and it was she who found the missing toddler. Gordon was searching along one bank, Mary along the other. She discovered the child lying face down in the river. Philomena had met her death by drowning, in a foot and a half of water.

Mary stood silently on the bank, looking down at the tiny corpse. Gordon saw she was very upset – as anybody would be. He climbed down, took Philomena in his arms and brought her to the Flynn house. The GP, Dr Phelan, was summoned and he examined the body. Though he noticed a slight discoloration of skin on the forehead, he attached no great significance to it.

That evening Michael Flynn returned home from the agricultural show in Rathdowney to find his wife close to a nervous breakdown and the farmhouse shrouded in mourning. Mary Cole seemed as upset as everybody else.

An inquest into the tragedy was held and the death pronounced accidental. This is surprising, given that the circumstances of the drowning were highly suspect. In order to reach the river she'd died in, the little girl would have had to do the following, alone and unaided. She'd have had to make her way through a dense thicket, climb over a barbed-wire fence and walk through a field where a crop of oats was growing. Towards the end of July the oats would have been a good head taller than Philomena.

There was only one other route; this would have led her through a gate into a field where the Flynns' cow was pastured. But there was an unusually thick growth of furze on the bank of the stream – all but impassable for a child of twenty-two months.

Mary Cole had an explanation of her own. There was the stump of an ash tree beside a shed on the near side of the barbed wire; it could be used as a step to enter the field. Mary offered the theory that Philomena had clambered over this. In fact the girl had seen the child in the same field a week before the tragedy; she'd been on an errand and returned just in time to spot Philomena going that way towards the river. She'd brought her back immediately, knowing that Mrs Flynn refused to have any of the children straying off on their own.

'Oh, my God!' the mother cried. 'Why didn't you tell me that at the time? I could have gone down there.'

Mary hadn't told her then. Nor had she told her that she'd been with Philomena around the time of her death. She'd been seen by two of the neighbours: John Hennessy, a farm labourer, and a girl called Mary Bastic.

Hennessy had been driving a cart along the main road at about a quarter to six that day. He happened to glance into Flynn's field and spotted Mary and Philomena; the child was wearing a red coat. Mary was driving the cow towards the gate and the toddler was running alongside. When next he saw Mary Cole she was in Phelan's shop buying linseed meal for the calf.

Mary Bastic had been going home with her brother and had seen Mary in the field as well. She could confirm that Philomena was with her – and wearing a red coat.

The coat was important. When the child was found in the water she wasn't wearing it. It was back at the Flynn home.

There was another nagging doubt. When Mrs Flynn came downstairs at six o'clock she'd asked Mary to milk the cow. At least two witnesses saw Mary driving the cow towards the house. Yet the girl hadn't told her employer that she'd already milked the animal.

Two further incidents were to blight Michael and Anastasia Flynn's lives the following month. The first was relatively minor compared to Philomena's death; all the same it was disturbing.

On 12 August Mrs Flynn returned from Phelan's shop. She'd given Kate Tobin, the other servant, the day off; her husband was away on business, and Mary was taking care of the two remaining children. They were playing in the yard under Mary's watchful eye.

Mrs Flynn smelled smoke on entering the kitchen. She ran to the parlour, to find a settee smouldering. She yelled for Mary and between them they managed to put out the fire before it could take proper hold. Another few seconds and the house might have gone up in flames.

Now settees do not, as a rule, spontaneously combust. There was a box of matches on the parlour floor and a number of spent matches lay scattered here and there. Mary, again, had an explanation ready to hand: six-year-old Maureen was fond of playing with matches. Time and again Mary had scolded her about this but the child continued to play with fire when she thought no one was looking. And Mary hadn't eyes in the back of her head, had she?

Mrs Flynn accepted this story with some reluctance. Though angry with both Mary and her daughter she was relieved that another calamity had been averted.

The second incident was infinitely more serious – the Flynns' eldest child drowned. The circumstances were so similar to the first tragedy that it's a wonder no suspicions were aroused at the time. To lose two children by drowning looked like more than carelessness on Mary's part.

The times of day were almost identical too. On 22 August Mrs Flynn was again resting upstairs; her husband was reading in the parlour. Shortly before half past five Mr Flynn glanced out of the window and saw Mary walking past the house carrying a bucket and heading towards the field where the cow was pastured. It was raining. He watched the girl pause on reaching the road, stand for a time, then go off in the direction of Phelan's shop. Flynn assumed she was going there to buy more meal for the calf; he was familiar with her routine. Some twenty minutes later he saw her again, this time leading the cow into the yard.

Upstairs Mrs Flynn heard the tolling of the angelus and came down to the kitchen. She found only Kate there together with her infant son Michael.

'Where's Maureen?' she asked. She had last seen her daughter at about half past five. The child had been carrying a kettle of water into the yard and calling after somebody; it could have been Kate, it could have been Mary.

But Kate didn't know where the child had got to; she'd

assumed she was in the parlour with her father.

Dread descended on Mrs Flynn; she panicked and started screaming. Her husband came rushing into the kitchen; Mary Cole, her milking of the cow completed, entered by the back-door.

'Have you seen Maureen?' Mr Flynn asked.

Mary had not. She told them she'd had difficulty finding the cow because it had strayed to the far end of the field. Maureen had wished to accompany her but Mary sent her home.

The parents and the two servants set off at once in the direction of the river. The Flynns dared not believe that a fate similar to Philomena's might have overtaken her sister. It was impossible.

Maureen, however, hadn't drowned in the river. Flynn found her lying face down in a stream, a tiny tributary of the Nore. The water was only eight or nine inches deep. Flynn turned the child over and saw that her face was red and there was froth around the mouth. She didn't appear to be breathing. He hurried with her to the house and laid her on a couch in the parlour. Only then did he notice a dark bruise on his little daughter's forehead.

He called in Dr Michael McCarthy, who examined the child. They were too late. Maureen was dead.

The doctor decided to subject the body to a thorough examination, and to hold an inquest. He concluded that the bruise to the forehead had been caused by a blunt object, possibly one of the stones on the bed of the stream where Flynn had found his daughter.

This time there was no one who could connect Mary with a child at the time of its death. True, a boy of thirteen had seen Maureen coming from her parents' home – and Mary leaving the house at the same time. But that was all. The same boy had milked the Flynns' cow. Mary had asked a neighbour to do it for her, and the neighbour had in turn entrusted the task to the boy.

If Mary hadn't been milking, then what *had* she been doing between five-thirty and six o'clock?

With only one child left to care for, the broken-hearted Flynns no longer needed two servants in the house. They decided to let Mary Cole go. By a happy coincidence Mary's mother was thinking of sending her to England at about this time; her sister-in-law had heard of a good opening in a department store that might suit Mary. Mrs Flynn hoped this decision had nothing to do with the tragedies; Mrs Cole assured her it had not.

Mary left the Flynns at the end of August. There were no recriminations because there were, as yet, no suspicions. In fact Mrs Flynn gave Mary a little present when seeing her off. She returned to her home in Mountrath.

Back in Rathdowney the gardaí, unsatisfied with the incredible 'coincidence' of the two children dying in almost identical circumstances, began to make inquiries. They interviewed the Flynns and Kate Tobin, each of whom seemed unsure of Mary's whereabouts and movements on the fateful days. They questioned the witnesses who'd seen Mary and the second child together – and concluded that she must have had a hand in the drownings. They alerted their colleagues in Mountrath.

Chief Superintendent Cooney knew Mary's parents. They were decent, hardworking people who'd expressed shock – if not surprise – on hearing of Mary's dalliance with the boys of Camross. He learned that Mary had always been 'a bit of a handful'.

Cooney paid a visit to the Coles' house on 3 October.

Mary was preparing to leave for England. She answered his questions with the same sullenness Mrs Flynn had noted. The chief superintendent already had several versions of the girl's comings and goings on the days in question, as reported by neighbours. They conflicted with Mary's version of events. Cooney left, but not before cautioning Mrs Cole to keep her daughter at home 'until certain matters have been cleared up'.

He was back on 14 November in the company of one of his sergeants. Cooney had asked the Rathdowney gardaí to go through the statements again and compare them with Mary's. They'd spoken to Dr Phelan and Dr McCarthy; both men had verified that the dead children had sustained similar injuries to the forehead – injuries that could have been incurred by their heads having been held against stones under the water.

Mary came back voluntarily to the barracks in Mountrath, where she made a second statement. There were more contradictions. Cooney arrested her.

William Carrigan, the senior state prosecutor, had no doubt at all that the court was dealing with a young monster. 'The girl in the dock', he told the jury in the Central Criminal Court, 'is a girl of an unnatural kind – a girl with a powerful but disordered intellect. One of the baffling proofs of her skill and unnatural ingenuity', he went on, 'is that neither the local police and doctors who attended the inquests on the children, nor the parents, for a moment suspected that the children had come to their end by anything else than the merest accident.'

He might also have said that Mary Cole, given her age, was about the most cold-blooded and heartless woman ever to appear in an Irish courtroom. While the other female killers in the pages of *Bloody Women* could have argued a certain justification for their terrible crimes, Mary's revenge was out of all proportion to the 'wrong' that had provoked it. The Flynns had shown her every kindness; Mrs Flynn had even made her a present of the navy-blue outfit and sweater. She'd taken the clothes back, and had informed the parish priest that Mary was misbehaving. And for these 'crimes' Mary had tried to burn the Flynns' house down – and drowned two innocent little children.

Carrigan wanted the death penalty; he felt that if anybody deserved it then it was Mary. But she was fifteen when the case came to court on 20 March 1928 and the death penalty could not be imposed on anyone under the age of sixteen.

Mary Cole pleaded not guilty to three counts: those of arson and the two murders. Following a legal wrangle the judge, Mr Justice O'Byrne, ruled that the arson indictment be dropped.

Witnesses were called in the course of the trial, which lasted for four days. Both Flynns gave evidence, as did the doctors who'd presided at the inquests.

John Hennessy and Mary Bastic, the neighbours who claimed to have seen Philomena in Mary Cole's company shortly before her death, restated that the child had been wearing a red coat. Mary swore that Mrs Flynn had given the coat to her to be washed that day; Mrs Flynn denied this. It was a minor point yet it was the first piece of contradictory evidence the jury was to hear.

Mary was shown to have lied about not having milked the cow that day – nor had she been busy milking the cow when Maureen met her death. The milking was her alibi on both occasions, and it was shown to be false.

The circumstantial evidence grew daily. The court was shown the virtual impossibility of little Philomena having made her way alone to the river; and the unlikelihood of Maureen having drowned in only eight or nine inches of water. Carrigan made much of Mary's 'milking' alibi.

'When you see the time and the nature of her duties when Philomena was drowned,' he asked the jury to consider, 'and compare them with the time and the nature of her duties at the time Maureen was drowned, you will see a link and a connection between the two crimes.'

Mary had been extremely clever, Carrigan said, but she'd made two fatal slips.

'Those were when she wilfully misplaced the position in the fields where she found the cow on each of the two occasions. Somebody placed the sturdy Maureen in the water and held her there until she became unconscious. Nobody had a motive for doing so except the accused.'

The servant Kate Tobin might not have been the most reliable of witnesses – at one point she told the court that at the time of the fire in the Flynns' home she'd seen a brush 'flying out the window'; at another she'd spoken of ghosts having taken the milk from the cow. Yet her testimony also contained points worth pondering. Mary had told her that Mrs Flynn was 'a hard woman to take away the costume she gave her'. And most damning of all were Mary's words to Kate: 'If Mrs Flynn brought the priest on me twice, she had two inquests in the house since.'

Mr Justice Byrne reminded the jurors that a conviction could be made only in the absence of all reasonable doubt. The jurors found no such absence. Mary Cole was found guilty and sentenced to life imprisonment.

Annie Walsh and the Husband
She Murdered for Love

They buried 'Sonny' Dan Walsh on the last day of May 1928. There was a good turnout for his funeral, for he was a well-liked farmer in Rosmuck, County Galway. (Many of us will recognize the place as the location of Padraic Pearse's summer cottage, where he penned verse, the lovely *Íosagán* and other stories.)

Walsh, aged fifty-six, left a grieving widow, Annie, two sons and a daughter – as well as three stepdaughters, the progeny of Annie's first marriage, in America, in 1914. She was thus widowed a second time.

As Walsh's coffin was lowered into the earth, the assembled mourners could not but notice the presence of a young man at Annie's side. This was a second cousin, Martin Joyce, aged twenty-five and a native of Rosmuck – and local rumour had it that the friendship between Annie and Martin was far from platonic. All Rosmuck was convinced they were lovers.

They exhumed the body of Sonny Dan Walsh on 28 November. The State Pathologist wished to examine it for traces of poison. It was too late: the soil of Connemara had done its work well and no such evidence was found.

Walsh's death had been an unorthodox one. Like the Flynn children, he'd drowned – in barely four inches of water. He'd been found lying face down in a tiny stream not far from his home. He might have fainted; he might have suffered a heart attack. He might also have been drunk because a five-naggin bottle of poteen was found in one of his pockets.

The State Pathologist had been looking for residues of poison for good reason: many people in the locality were convinced that Annie Walsh had done away with her husband. And poison was generally regarded as the weapon of choice of the female killer.

The Guards, however, had nothing but rumour to support the theory of foul play. Rumour that may well have been no more than malicious gossip.

The problem was that the people of Rosmuck had a soft spot for Sonny, and refused to allow his death to go unchallenged. He was regarded as a 'quiet man' – rural shorthand for a simple soul. Sonny had suffered severe burns in a childhood accident that left him mentally deficient. He was also known to be a heavy drinker; sometimes neighbours had to carry him home unconscious, following a night's carousing. The bottle of poteen found in his pocket gave credence to the theory that immoderate drinking had contributed to his death.

Yet the poteen hadn't been touched – therefore the notion that a drunken Sonny had staggered at the water's edge, slipped, fallen into the stream, hit his head, lost consciousness and drowned in only four inches of water, hardly held much water itself.

Certainly it was possible; such freak accidents occur. Rumour, however, had it that Sonny's wife had been trying to get him out of the way. There was dark talk of the amorous relationship with the younger man, the close relative: Martin Joyce.

Thus were the gardaí obliged to go back over what they knew of the circumstances surrounding Sonny's death. They were these.

That day, a Wednesday, Sonny had spent working on his small-holding. He'd come back to the house at suppertime, had a bite to eat and put his younger children to bed.

That done, he left the house again, this time to walk to the town of Oughterard. It lay thirteen miles distant as the crow flies; but Sonny was on foot and Rosmuck lies at the southern end of a small peninsula. Even allowing for the short cuts Sonny knew, the distance would have been at least twenty miles. It was going to be an all-night hike, there and back.

His purpose was to have a crib – or framework – made for a cart. His wife Annie told the police she'd given him thirty shillings with which to pay for it. She hadn't expected him to return before daybreak. The first she knew of his death was when the authorities notified her early on the Thursday morning.

There was some bruising to Sonny's head and face. The wounds were minor, consistent with his having fallen on the pebbles in the stream and knocking himself unconscious. The coroner found water in the lungs, indicating that the man had been alive when the water entered through his nose and mouth. Death from 'asphyxia due to accidental drowning' was the verdict.

There was also another matter to consider. Annie had given her husband thirty shillings to pay for the crib; no money was found on his person and there was no sign of a crib. Only a bottle of poteen. Had Sonny squandered the money on a night's drinking with a person or persons unknown? The presence of the poteen could account for such an eventuality – and everybody knew Sonny's reputation as a drunkard.

As the months passed, local talk of Sonny's death didn't diminish; it grew. There was great indignation among those who'd known the dead man: nobody was happy with the coroner's verdict.

Nor was interest confined to Connemara. Two of Sonny's sisters lived in the United States. On learning of his death – and the suspicions of the people of Rosmuck – they approached a nephew of Sonny's who worked as a lawyer. He in turn contacted the Irish Department of Justice, and succeeded in having the case reopened.

The gardaí in Dublin dispatched two of their best men to investigate: Superintendent James Hunt and Detective Sergeant George Lawlor. The latter would distinguish himself in the decades to come, not least as head of the Garda Technical Bureau, established in 1934.

Arriving in Rosmuck the detectives began, not unnaturally, by questioning Sonny's widow – and the man who'd started the tongues wagging: Martin Joyce. It was a slow process because the pair, in common with most people in the area, spoke no English and could relate their stories only through interpreters.

Joyce had a cast-iron alibi for the night of Sonny's drowning. He'd gone to Inishmore, the largest of the Aran Islands, to attend a funeral. Inishmore lies about thirteen miles from Rosmuck, and almost due south. But to get there you have to cross two stretches of water. Joyce related how he made the first crossing in his own boat, then employed the services of a ferryman for the actual sea journey.

He'd attended the funeral, he said, and joined the islanders at the wake, during which he drank heavily. He arrived back in Rosmuck sometime in the afternoon of Thursday, 31 May, the day Sonny's body was found.

Joyce could recall his movements in minute detail – and this six months after the drowning. The difficulty was that no one whom the detectives interviewed on Inishmore could remember Joyce's having been there at all – and the wake had actually been held on 29 May, a day earlier than Joyce had stated. More damningly, a Rosmuck man, John Walsh, had seen Joyce in the locality at the time he claimed to have been on Inishmore.

Walsh was a nephew of Sonny Dan's. He told the gardaí that at about eleven o'clock on the Wednesday night his dog had begun to bark. He'd looked out of the window and spotted Joyce walking past – in the company of his uncle Sonny. Walsh was adamant about the identity of the men; the moon that night was almost full and visibility was excellent.

Martin Joyce was becoming the prime suspect in a case the police were increasingly coming to regard as murder.

Joyce and Annie, for their part, were growing increasingly concerned for their safety. They'd known about the rumours following hard on the death of Annie's husband. They knew the rumours had gathered momentum and the exhumation of the corpse had added fuel to their fears.

The truth was that Joyce and Annie had become lovers long before Sonny's death. Sonny was fond of cards and often invited the neighbours round for a few hands and a bottle or two. Joyce was a regular visitor.

Annie sometimes joined in a game of cards herself, and it was not unknown for Joyce and her to continue playing until late at night, after her husband had gone to bed. In all probability it was during one such late-night session that Annie's love affair with the twenty-five-year-old began. And so it was that, from time to time, Joyce would let himself out of the house in the early morning before his host awoke. . . .

Life can't have been easy for Annie. The card evenings would have given her some respite from the drudgery of marriage to a poor farmer in a remote part of Connemara. She'd had a taste of life in the United States and therefore was aware of the wide world beyond Rosmuck. Joyce was as determined as she to quit the district and make a fresh start. Canada was his goal.

You might be forgiven for thinking you'd strayed into a play by John Millington Synge. The characters are there: the aging farmer, his younger wife – and the still-younger lover who wishes to deliver her from a drab existence in one of Ireland's most remote localities, and whisk her off to a life of adventure. You can imagine that Annie's thoughts, as she contemplated the prospect of remaining with her unloving husband, and watching the wind and rain sweep in from the Atlantic, were not unlike those of Nora in *The Shadow of the Glen*.

> I do be thinking in the long nights it was a big fool I was [to marry her husband Dan] . . . for what good is a bit of a farm with cows on it, and sheep on the back hills, when you do be sitting, looking out from a door . . . and seeing nothing but the mists rolling down the bog, and the mists again, and they rolling up

the bog, and hearing nothing but the wind crying out in the bits of broken trees were left from the great storm, and the streams roaring with the rain?

Sonny's house was little more than a hovel: three tiny rooms and a kitchen that looked out over a dirt yard. There weren't even enough beds in the place to go round. Beyond the yard was a barren waste devoid of trees. Rough tracks strewn with stones were the cottage's sole link with civilization.

The solitude that Padraic Pearse sought and found in Rosmuck was Annie's daily lot. He chose it; she didn't. She'd left the USA and returned to County Galway with three daughters in tow. Penniless and landless, her only hope of security had been to marry Sonny. Anything was preferable to the poorhouse – even a loveless marriage in the wasteland that was Rosmuck.

The garda investigation gave renewed impetus to Martin Joyce's plan to emigrate. He made arrangements to flee the country – alone.

Annie, meanwhile, was having trouble with her own household. In her statement to the gardaí she'd claimed that Joyce hadn't been in her home on the night of the murder. She'd also said that she herself hadn't left the house. This latter assertion was contradicted by her fourteen-year-old daughter Mary.

Annie panicked. She feared the police might also question Rita, aged ten, who was even more of a chatterbox, so she packed the girl off to the Aran Islands. The Guards discovered her whereabouts and questioned her there. Rita informed them that Joyce had been in her dead stepfather's home on the night of 30 May.

To further add to Annie's troubles the detectives who'd remained in Rosmuck were interviewing the neighbours. Some of them badmouthed Annie and Joyce, claiming that the suspects were in the habit of making disparaging remarks about Sonny Walsh after he'd gone to bed early on card nights.

Her children were also saying more than they should have. From them the investigators gleaned the knowledge that Joyce and Annie had planned marriage – Joyce had actually told the children that the marriage had already taken place. The detectives learned that Joyce had lain low for a month after the funeral. He'd returned to the house and moved into Annie's bed, hiding in the loft during the day and emerging in the evening.

The couple were arrested. The case was heard first in the District Court; the trial proper began in the Central Criminal Court on 18 June 1929.

Annie's children were to prove her undoing. When the detectives questioned them in Connemara it was obvious that Mary, Catherine and Rita lived in fear of their mother. Now, in the courtroom – with a phalanx of interpreters standing by to translate their testimony into English – the girls seemed happy to unburden themselves of the secrets they shared with Annie and her lover.

It soon became clear to the jury that Annie had been making plans for a future that didn't include Sonny. Joyce was earmarked as the 'coming man'; she'd sent her children to buy presents for him on several occasions. She'd sketched for them a scenario wherein Sonny was dead and Joyce had assumed the father role. Annie had gone to great lengths to convince the children that their lives would be so much better with Joyce in Sonny's place.

Mary told the court what had happened the day before her stepfather's death. Annie sent her to buy a bottle of poteen. When she returned in the afternoon Joyce was drunk and sharing Annie's bedroom. Sonny came home some time later and was plied with poteen. When he left the house that night to go to Oughterard, he was very drunk indeed.

Mary went to bed. She awoke in the middle of the night to find Annie and Joyce in her bedroom. They'd come in through the window, so as not to rouse the whole house. Joyce told the girl of an argument he'd had with her drunken stepfather – how Sonny had produced a knife and threatened to kill him. Annie and Joyce had left him raving on the roadside. Mary saw that both her mother's and Joyce's clothes and boots were wet and muddied.

Mary confirmed that which the detectives had suspected: she and Annie's other children had been beaten into submission, had been told to lie to the police and to the magistrate at the District Court. Now the floodgates were open.

The prosecutor called another witness: a neighbour, Martin Conroy, who'd spoken with Joyce after Sonny's death.

'Nothing can be said to me when nobody saw me do it,' Joyce reputedly said to him.

It was Annie's turn to give evidence. She clarified her relationship with Martin Joyce, claiming he was no more than a person who sometimes worked for her late husband. Joyce had not, she said, been given special treatment – she'd never given him gifts. He'd sometimes slept in the house, with Sonny's blessing. And yes, he *had* been in the house on the night of Sonny's death.

Sonny and Martin Joyce had drunk poteen that night.

Annie, having put the children to bed at nine o'clock, retired herself at ten or thereabouts. Joyce had agreed to accompany Sonny to Oughterard and the pair set off together. That was the last time she saw her husband alive. She was thereby contradicting her daughter Mary's story of her having left the house that night, to return at a later hour with Joyce, with mud on her boots.

Had she planned on marrying Joyce and emigrating to Canada? Had she slept with him? Annie denied ever having had an affair with Joyce. The prosecutor wasn't satisfied.

'Are the children speaking false when they say you slept with Martin Joyce?' he asked.

'They are,' she replied. 'I had no reason to sleep with him. I would not go with him, having a man of my own.'

Nor had Joyce been in the house for weeks on end following the drowning.

'I never saw him there more than once or twice after my husband's death,' she said.

Joyce was called to the stand and he corroborated Annie's testimony. As regards the events of the fateful night: he had indeed agreed to accompany Sonny on his journey to Oughterard – but had gone only part of the way. They'd parted company after a few minutes and Joyce had set out for the wake on Aran.

Annie Walsh and Martin Joyce had planned the murder well. So well, in fact, that all evidence presented by the prosecution was circumstantial. Had Annie left the house that night? She swore she hadn't; her daughter swore she had. Had Joyce been with Sonny at the time of his death? He swore he'd been on his way to Inishmore; others say they saw him in Rosmuck when he ought to have been a great many miles away.

In fact the detectives had nothing to go on, save the thirty shillings Annie had given her husband that night and which wasn't found on the corpse. Annie suggested that Sonny might have lost the money on the way. He might equally have fallen prey to a robber.

The murder itself was an uncomplicated affair; it was as easy to drown Sonny Walsh as it was for Mary Cole to drown Mrs Flynn's children. He'd been very drunk – that part of the evidence was never in dispute – and might very well have slipped on some wet stones when passing the stream. He might have fallen heavily, to end up lying face down in the water. He might have lost consciousness and drowned accidentally.

The judge, Mr Justice O'Byrne, didn't think so. He was convinced that another person or persons had helped Sonny into the hereafter. The two most likely suspects stood before him in the court. Both had had mud on their clothing and footwear; both had lied. 'What can they say to me when they did not see me do it?' Joyce had asked a neighbour.

Whether Joyce alone had killed Sonny or whether Annie had had a hand in it, the jury could not say. But they found both guilty of murder. Justice O'Byrne addressed Joyce first.

'It is ordered and adjudged that you, Martin Joyce,' he said, 'be taken from the bar of the court where you now stand to the prison from where you last came, and that on Thursday, the eighteenth day of July, in the year of Our Lord nineteen hundred and twenty-nine, you be taken to the common place of execution in the prison in which you shall then be confined, and that you be then and there hanged by the neck until you be dead, and that your body be buried within the walls of the prison in which the aforesaid judgement of death shall be executed upon you.'

Joyce screamed as he was escorted below. It was Annie's turn to hear a similar sentence: she too was to die on 18 July. Unlike Joyce, she accepted her fate in silence.

They were spared the hangman's rope, however, following an appeal. Both received a reduced sentence, to life imprisonment.

Jane O'Brien, the Aunt with the Shotgun

Michael Fitzpatrick pushed up the brim of his hat, in defiance of the rain that was falling on the Republican Plot in Crosstown Cemetery, Enniscorthy. It was Easter Sunday, 27 March 1932, and Fitzpatrick was addressing the large crowd that had gathered to honour the Wexfordmen who'd fallen in 1916 and in the troubled years that followed.

'I want everyone here,' he declared, 'whether friends or enemies, to understand that the Irish Republican Army never unnecessarily shed blood. They have been on the defensive for the past ten years and any action they've taken has been taken in self-defence. The organization had no hand, act or part in, or knowledge of, the regrettable incident that occurred last night. I and my comrades here have no knowledge of how the occurrence came about. We certainly hope for the sake of the good name of County Wexford that it was an accident.'

The 'regrettable incident' was the gunning down in cold blood of John Cousins, thirty-two, of Killinick, then a tiny village near Rosslare. The shooting had the hallmarks of an IRA assassination. Cousins had been felled by a blast from a shotgun fired at close range, a little way inside the gates of his home, Sanctuary. Suspicion was compounded by the fact that for two weeks prior to the shooting persons unknown had hung warning notices along the driveway leading to the house. They read: *Informers Beware! IRA.*

These were dangerous times in Wexford – and indeed in the whole country. Fianna Fáil had won the general election on 9 March, returning seventy-two deputies. For the first time since their founding in 1926 they were in government, with Eamon de Valera at the helm; a coalition formed with seven Labour TDs gave Fianna Fáil a majority in the Dáil. Cumann na nGaedheal, the party that had been in power since 1923, suffered its first major defeat.

John Cousins of Sanctuary had acted as a personation agent for Cumann na nGaedheal. It was this which made supposed IRA threats against him seem credible: he was clearly hostile to every kind of republicanism and an ardent supporter of the old regime. He could be described as being a marked man. . . .

It was early in 1931 when Jane O'Brien learned that her nephew, John Cousins, had become engaged to a local girl, Annie McGuire. The news filled her with dread. She was in no doubt that she'd lose the roof over her head, that sooner of later she'd have to leave Sanctuary forever.

Jane was sixty and virtually penniless. To be sure, she had a son – also called John – living in the same house, so wouldn't be completely alone to fend for herself. But John's income was tiny: he worked for a pittance on a neighbouring farm and could hardly support himself, let alone two people. Jane foresaw a dismal future, either living in a poorhouse or going 'to the road': tramping the county in all weathers with her son.

The house called Sanctuary had once been her family home. It was a two-storey thatched farmhouse in Tudor style; from the late seventeenth century on, it had housed successive rectors of the Reformed Church. The farm itself was small – less than six acres – and at odds with the big gate and driveway that led to the house.

Jane married in 1899 and left Sanctuary to live with her husband, Andrew O'Brien. Money was tight: Andrew's job with the railway wasn't a well-paying one and the couple lived in a tiny cottage in Yoletown, close to Rosslare, where their son John was born.

Jane's brother William had inherited Sanctuary. In 1920 he approached Andrew and her with a proposal. His wife had died that year, leaving him alone on the farm with their only son, John, then aged twenty. Knowing Jane's circumstances he invited her to move back into the house, bringing with her her husband and son.

It was a very good arrangement for all concerned: the O'Briens would have a better roof over their heads; Sanctuary would acquire another pair of hands to work the farm and the house would again have a mistress to run it. Jane agreed at once. Andrew put the cottage in Yoletown up for sale; the modest proceeds were to be invested in Sanctuary.

Yet the move was a blow to Andrew O'Brien's pride; he'd failed as a husband and provider. His bitterness grew. Eventually he could stand it no longer and in 1927 he left Jane and his son, ostensibly to seek work in Scotland. In reality he was deserting them. Throughout that year and the following one he continued to write to his wife, and send a little money now and then. Jane saw him for the last time in May 1929. He had, he told her, found work in London and would forward money in due course so that his wife and son could join him there. It was a lie. She never heard from him again.

Jane settled into her now-altered role at Sanctuary, bringing up her boy and keeping house for her brother William. But he died in December 1931. He'd neglected to make a will and the property passed automatically to his son John, his sole heir. Jane, of course, received nothing and was left moreover in a highly vulnerable position. Should her nephew marry then she'd have to move out again because in those times – and indeed the situation obtains even today in some rural areas – it was accepted that a woman such as Jane must make way for the new mistress of the house. It was only a matter of time before Jane O'Brien found herself homeless.

There was a further injustice. What little money the sale of the cottage in Yoletown raised had been invested in Sanctuary and she'd see no return on it – or indeed on her years of hard work there.

And it *was* hard work keeping the place going. The farm was small; its annual yield was barely sufficient to sustain three people. When John Cousins was old enough he went to work as a labourer on the farm of a Mr White of Ballyrane. This he continued to do until 1931, when he found similar though more lucrative employment in the nearby townland of Ballysheen. Jane's son John took over Cousins's old job on White's farm.

John Cousins's change of employer wasn't a move he'd made lightly. He needed money. He was in the habit of visiting the home of a neighbour, William McGuire, a stone's throw from Sanctuary. He used to play cards with members of the McGuire family and friends from the neighbourhood, interrupting the games to drink a few pints of porter at Treacy's pub in the village of Killinick.

McGuire had a daughter, Annie, who was eleven years younger than Cousins. Before long, Jane O'Brien heard the news she'd dreaded: her nephew announced his engagement to the girl early in 1931.

The couple planned on marrying at Christmas. But Jane's brother William died on 14 December and it would not have been seemly to proceed with the wedding. So Cousins postponed it until the following June.

Aunt Jane spent the worst Christmas of her life. On the death of her brother she knew her days at Sanctuary were numbered. She'd be on the roads in less than six months. Drastic measures were called for.

We have no evidence that Jane O'Brien decided on murder so early in the year – or indeed that she contemplated violence of any sort. Her first acts appear to have been those of a desperate and frightened woman. She began sending anonymous picture postcards to Annie McGuire, her nephew's fiancée. They were saucy seaside cards replete with small men, and large women with overdeveloped bottoms. *Dear Annie*, Jane would write, *this fat behind reminds me of yours!*

Annie showed the cards to her fiancé. They laughed about them. John more than Annie – he was convinced that he had a secret admirer in the locality, one who resented his forthcoming marriage to Annie. It was a flattering thought. The couple told no one else about the cards.

But Jane was careless. She made no secret of her animosity towards Annie McGuire. On one occasion, when visiting the McGuire house, she saw Annie arranging her hair at a mirror. 'Are you doing yourself up to go with the old man?' she asked, the 'old man' being John Cousins.

On another occasion Annie went to the post office and found Jane chatting with the postmistress. As soon as the girl came in Jane hurried to leave.

'I'd better run now,' she said, 'or Annie'll think I'm the one who's sending those letters.'

It was a remark that showed her hand. Unlike Cousins, Annie had suspected Jane of sending the postcards. And they'd told nobody else about them.

Again, we don't know when the idea of murder entered Jane's head. We can only conjecture that, as the date of the wedding approached, her desperation grew. She must surely have discussed her future with her nephew – it would be odd indeed had they not spoken about it. Both knew that Jane O'Brien would have to leave Sanctuary.

We have only a statement made by Jane to the police the day after Cousins's murder. In it she avers that John threatened *her* with the shotgun and we've only her word to go on that this was the case. Nevertheless it gives an indication that feelings were running high in the house.

'The trouble started about a fortnight ago,' she stated. 'John Cousins lived with me for the past twelve years and was the owner of this place. When he'd finished shaving on Saturday evening, he said to me: "Jane, you'll have to be out of this in a week."

'I said: "What have I done to deserve this? What's the matter? After my twelve years, after all my expense, after all the money I left here. I'm not going out of the house until I've been compensated for what I've done."'

'Who asked you to do it?' John responded.

Then Jane made mention of a gun. Exactly why is unclear, though she might have been daring him to shoot her. Another explanation is that Jane was threatening to go to the authorities about the gun. John was holding it illegally; moreover possession of a firearm in those troubled times might have been construed as IRA involvement.

'Now, John,' she said, 'you can take that gun from where you have it hid.'

'Don't you ever split about that gun,' he's supposed to have said. 'If you do, I'll give you the contents of it.'

To which Aunt Jane replied: 'John, you'll never get the chance to give me the contents of it.'

Whatever really happened, whatever rows took place, Jane began her preparations. She knew Cousins owned a gun: a single-barrelled, breech-loading shotgun. It was in his room, possibly hidden between the mattresses on his bed. Jane kept house, therefore it's not improbable that she'd chanced upon the weapon while tidying his room. The cartridges might have been concealed alongside the gun, or close by.

Jane had the weapon. Now she needed a ruse to divert suspicion away from her. The general election provided her with one. John had angered the IRA by working as a personation agent; his aunt decided to fabricate a death threat from that organization. She slipped out at night and posted warnings along the driveway leading to the house. *Informers Beware!*

Then she went to work, arranging the ambush. At about five in the evening of Good Friday, 25 March, she took a handsaw from an outhouse and went down to the front gate – not by way of the avenue itself but through the field belonging to William Kelly, the next-door neighbour.

There were whitethorn hedges growing on either side of the avenue and at the point she chose, just inside the gate, they were some eight feet in height. Jane began to saw. Her object was to make a gap in the hedge.

She was busily sawing away at the whitethorn when a neighbour, Johanna Moran, happened along the road, and stopped to say hello. Fortunately for Jane, the hedge blocked Mrs Moran's view and she couldn't see the saw. She did, however, see 'something in her hand'. For some reason she thought Jane was using a hammer.

In fact Jane had chosen this spot because it gave her a sight on one of the gateposts – the one a person would pass in front of when returning to Sanctuary from the direction of the McGuire house.

The white posts now gleamed more whitely than ever; Jane had repainted them a few days before. The nights were relatively bright – the moon, full on Tuesday, still shed a good deal of light – but it had rained nightly since the beginning of Holy Week and clouds might obscure the moon. Jane had to be sure of drawing a good bead on her target. She was confident that the figure of a man walking past the gatepost would be silhouetted quite satisfactorily. . . .

The McGuires threw a party on Easter Saturday, principally in celebration of the impending marriage of their daughter to John Cousins.

Jane's son John was also invited. But he declined; he'd planned on spending the evening at the cinema with his girlfriend. On returning from work on White's farm, he had something to eat, shaved, then set off on his bicycle for Wexford town. It was shortly after 7 p.m. and he left his mother alone in the house with her nephew.

But not for long. John Cousins had some chores to do before the party. He cleaned out the donkey shed and tended to the ponies. Then he set out for the McGuires', having first asked Jane to 'have something nice for the supper' on his return.

Jane hurried upstairs to her nephew's bedroom. She took the shotgun from its hiding place and loaded it with a 12-bore cartridge, stuffing another into her blouse.

The party at the McGuire house was slow to start; when John Cousins arrived at 8.30 there were only three guests present. One was Jemmy O'Reilly, a friend and neighbour. He and John decided to repair to Mrs Treacy's public house in Killinick. They had a few drinks there, then went their separate ways, to meet later back at the party; O'Reilly had some business to attend to.

Jane O'Brien waited in the dark behind the whitethorn hedge inside the gate of Sanctuary, the shotgun resting on a Y-shaped piece of cut briar. She'd no idea how long the party might last, though she could be pretty certain that Cousins would return before midnight; she'd heard him tell her son he was going to watch the Easter procession the following morning. And we can only guess how she must have felt as she prepared to kill the inoffensive man whose only 'crime' was his adherence to family custom. By her own admission she'd never used a weapon before and here she was, sighting through the hole she'd sawn in the hedge as the rain began to fall from an overcast sky.

It was only 250 yards to the McGuire house – so close in fact that Jane might have heard the neighbour's door slam shut at about 11.30, the time Jemmy O'Reilly and her nephew left the party. She might even have heard their footsteps approaching on the road, and words they exchanged.

She heard Jemmy O'Reilly bid her nephew goodnight as they came to the gate. Jemmy walked on towards his own home. Then John Cousins was passing in front of the gatepost. . . .

O'Reilly heard the shotgun blast and turned. It appeared to have come from the direction of the church adjacent to his friend's property. He turned back.

John Cousins was approaching at an awkward run. His body was doubled over.

'Oh, Jemmy,' he cried. 'I'm shot!'

Thinking rapidly, O'Reilly reasoned that Sanctuary provided no sanctuary for his wounded friend. Whoever had fired the shot might still be skulking there. He put an arm around the wounded Cousins and helped him along the road in the direction of the next dwelling: that of Robert Rowe. But John was near to collapse. He fell onto the roadway a few yards from the cottage.

Jane O'Brien had an escape route planned; it led her back past the tall whitethorn hedge that skirted Kelly's field. She picked her way in the dark and found the gap in the hedge, about eighty yards from the site of ambush, climbed through it and slithered down onto the avenue leading to Sanctuary.

There was nothing – as far as she knew – that would link her to the attack on her nephew. But the police might search Cousins's room for clues to the motive. They'd find the shotgun. So she hid it between the mattresses of her own bed. That done, she undressed and pulled on her night attire.

Jemmy O'Reilly in the meantime was doing his utmost for his fallen friend. Having left Cousins propped against a gatepost outside their cottage, he'd roused the Rowe household. He'd then run to William Kelly's house; Kelly, he knew, could alert both the parish priest and the local GP, Dr Henry Anglim.

Next, O'Reilly had to get to a telephone; the gardaí must be summoned – for all he knew the whole neighbourhood might be in danger. The nearest phone was in the post office. There was a short cut, but taking it meant scrambling over a wall on Kelly's property. When doing so he fell heavily and hurt himself more than he knew. By the time he reached the post office and roused the postmistress his injuries had got the better of him; he fainted. But he'd succeeded in getting the message through.

Guard Grimes and Sergeant Hanley of Rosslare garda station arrived at the Rowe cottage at ten minutes to one. Inexplicably, John Cousins was still outside where his friend had left him, though somebody had swathed him in several overcoats. The rain had increased.

The Rowe family and others from the neighbourhood were gathered about the wounded man. Father Murphy, the parish priest, had been at the scene for some time, though there was no talk yet of the last rites.

John O'Brien, Jane's son, was there as well, having cycled back from Wexford town.

Grimes knew the victim well and recognized him at once. He saw that Cousins was in great pain; he was lying on his back, groaning and kicking. One of the neighbours was doing his utmost to stanch the wound.

The Guard made a cursory examination; despite the loss of blood, he didn't believe the shotgun wound was life-threatening. He was more concerned with the facts surrounding the assault.

'John,' he said, 'I'm Guard Grimes. How many shots were fired?'

John told him. Grimes accepted a small bottle of whiskey from one of the concerned neighbours and offered some to Cousins. He refused; he was unable to drink it.

Perhaps this fact should have alerted the police officer to the seriousness of Cousins's injuries but this was not so. Indeed Dr Anglim arrived on the scene at about this time, examined the injured man and failed to note that Cousins was very close to death. There were a number of small puncture wounds to the stomach, scattered over an area of about five square inches. Cousins had been shot at close range, was bleeding profusely and drifting in and out of consciousness.

Anglim was a competent physician – as his testimony showed. The question arises: Why did he allow Cousins to lie outdoors in the rain and cold, and not attempt immediate emergency treatment, either in Sanctuary, in the Rowe cottage, or in his own surgery?

In the event Anglim directed that Cousins be removed to hospital without delay, and transport was ordered.

It was 1.20 a.m. when the car set out for the County Hospital in Wexford. The victim had lain haemorrhaging for almost two hours.

Sergeant Hanley sat in the back-seat with Cousins, cradling his head and making him as comfortable as possible. John O'Brien accompanied them.

Wexford was no more than a ten-minute drive away, therefore Cousins might have survived. But ill luck intervened: two miles from the hospital a tyre punctured.

'Proceed on the rim!' Sergeant Hanley ordered.

The driver refused. He feared the wheel might break. Instead he strove to mend the puncture in the pouring rain. Cousins regained consciousness again at this time.

'I'm dying, I'm dying,' he moaned. 'Oh, the pain!'

He begged Hanley to make him more comfortable on the seat. But it was too late. Within minutes he was dead, as a result of shock and loss of blood. At 2.30 the car, when it finally arrived in Wexford, contained a corpse.

John Cousins was, to those who knew him, 'a quiet and inoffensive man and most popular in the district'. To Superintendent Halloran's knowledge, the victim had not belonged to an illegal organization and had no enemies. Halloran also ruled out theft as a motive: when he examined the body at the hospital he saw that Cousins's purse was untouched. As was his watch; it had been damaged in places by shotgun pellets.

The clue to the murder might be found in Sanctuary. Halloran was joined by Sergeant Hanley and a body of Guards, and they arrived at the house shortly after four in the morning. John O'Brien followed in the car that had brought his dead cousin to the hospital.

The house was in darkness. Jane, dressed in her night-clothes, a lighted candle in her hand, opened the door. Sergeant Hanley noticed that she began to 'whimper or sob', though there were no tears. He grew suspicious; as far as he was aware, nobody had sent word to Jane that her nephew had been shot.

'What's happened?' she asked.

'Don't be frightened. There's been an accident.'

Jane was distressed. Her eye fell on her son John.

'An accident, an accident!' she exclaimed. 'Oh, what's wrong with you, John?'

'John's all right,' Hanley said. 'But your nephew John Cousins has met with an accident.'

The Guards followed Jane into the kitchen. She lit a lamp and turned again to Sergeant Hanley.

'Where did it happen?'

'In the village.'

'An accident, an accident,' Jane said again. 'Was it a motor car?'

Hanley didn't answer. He was mentally sifting through certain items of information surrounding the case. Already he suspected Jane's involvement.

Item: He knew about the postcards John Cousins and his fiancée had received and Jane's strange words to the postmistress.

Item: He also knew about the threatening notices that had appeared during the run-up to the election, and was convinced they were bogus.

Item: Jane had begun to sob *before* hearing the news of Cousins's death.

'Poor John,' she said then. 'What happened to him at all, poor fella? I'm only after getting up after an attack of influenza. The poor fella! The last thing he said to me tonight going out was to have something nice for him for supper.' She pointed to the kitchen table; there were two places laid. 'I had the supper ready for the two boys.'

Halloran noticed that she asked nothing about John's injuries. It would have been the natural thing to do.

It was at this point that her son suddenly became hysterical. No doubt he was beginning to appreciate the seriousness of the situation: his cousin had been murdered, almost on his own doorstep. Who knew who'd be next? John O'Brien read the papers, was aware of the residual, violent legacy of the Troubles and the civil war. As the Guards were leaving, he rushed to one and flung his arms around the startled man's neck.

'Don't go!' he pleaded. 'Leave somebody with us.'

'Have sense, John,' Sergeant Hanley chided. 'Don't be frightening your mother.'

But Superintendent Halloran took the cue and decided

to remain a little longer. He asked Jane to show them her nephew's room, explaining that it might contain clues – perhaps threatening letters Cousins had received.

Halloran and Hanley made a thorough search of the room – one of three bedrooms having interconnecting doors. The superintendent didn't inform Jane at the time that he was looking for a gun. They turned over the mattresses on the dead man's bed but found nothing.

It was a quarter to five when they finally left the house. An officer was posted at the gate, much to John O'Brien's relief. He still believed that his cousin had been gunned down by the IRA. Superintendent Halloran, however, had other thoughts: Jane had asked nothing more about her nephew's condition, nor had she expressed a desire to see him.

The officers went to Killinick, where Halloran telephoned his superior, Chief Superintendent McCarthy. He returned to Sanctuary at first light, accompanied by his sergeant.

It was Sergeant Hanley who found the first piece of evidence, lying just inside the gate. It was a wad and cartridge case, ejected from a shotgun. There were pellets embedded in one of the gateposts.

The trajectory led the officers to the field owned by the neighbour and it was here, behind the tall hedge, that they came upon a patch of grass and primroses that had been trampled on – as though somebody had stood there for a time. They also found traces of freshly broken ivy.

A swift search of the hedge revealed Jane's handiwork. The officers found the place where the whitethorn had been sawn through. It gave a clear sight on the gatepost.

But the attacker hadn't entered from the road, Halloran discovered. Some distance from the ambush site, close to the house, he found a break in the fence and signs that the assailant had used it. There were no tracks in Kelly's field – despite the continuous rain which would have softened the earth. Clearly the murderer had come from the direction of the house.

John O'Brien was in the yard, preparing food for the pigs. His mother was in the kitchen. She wore a cloth around her head and explained that this was because of a headache. Halloran suggested she'd better lie down, and took a statement from her son as he awaited the arrival of his superior.

Chief Superintendent McCarthy showed up at eight o'clock, accompanied by a body of Guards and several detectives. McCarthy asked John if there was a saw on the property. There was; John produced one from an out-house. It had been used recently: fresh sawdust clung to the teeth.

Jane was summoned. Had she used the saw? She had not. Had John Cousins used it? She couldn't remember.

Then McCarthy confronted her with his suspicions.

'Now, Mrs O'Brien,' he said, 'I believe the gun that murdered John Cousins is concealed in this house. Before you answer any other questions I put to you in connection with the murder, I would like you to consider your answers carefully because what you say may be used in evidence afterwards.'

McCarthy was direct: 'Where is the gun that murdered John Cousins?'

'There's no gun in this house and I never saw one. Surely you don't say I know anything about the murder of John Cousins. You can search the place again.'

McCarthy did just that. He sent Jane to her room and had his men conduct a search of the ground floor, then the victim's bedroom, as well as an attic directly above it.

McCarthy was convinced that Jane O'Brien was lying. The gun, he thought, might be anywhere, yet he felt certain it was in her room. Deliberately he'd left that room till last. He joined her there.

'I know the gun is here,' he said. 'Hand it over and save yourself and us the trouble of further search.'

'The gun, the gun, the gun,' Jane said. 'I know nothing about it. I know nothing about it. There used to be rumours that John Cousins had a gun but I never saw it.'

McCarthy continued his bluff.

'We know the person that cut the bush in the laneway,' he told her. 'We know all. You'd better tell us all about it.'

'There's no gun here,' she maintained. 'I never saw a gun here.'

But Jane's eyes had betrayed her. McCarthy caught her gaze returning again and again to her bed. He ordered his men to search it. Sure enough, concealed between two of the three mattresses was a single action, breech-loading fowling piece.

Halloran opened the breech. The shotgun smelled strongly of burnt powder. He sighted through the barrel and knew the gun had been fired recently.

The game was up and Jane knew it. She broke.

'I'll tell you all about it,' she said.

The trial of Jane O'Brien aroused great interest in Wexford – in particular among the women of the county. Hundreds gathered outside the District Courthouse and those unable to gain admission waited for the first day's hearing to end so they might catch a glimpse of the tall sixty-year-old who'd been charged with the murder of her own nephew.

It must be said of Jane's defence counsel, Albert Wood, that he put up a good fight against the odds. He attempted to have the statement taken by Chief Superintendent McCarthy thrown out on the grounds that Jane hadn't been cautioned properly before making it. There were other discrepancies, he argued, in the depositions made by McCarthy's colleagues.

But what could not be laid aside by references to arcane legal precedents ('I will give this authority: *Archibald*, nineteen twenty-seven edition,' offered Jane's defence counsel at one stage) was the damning fact that the murder weapon had been found concealed in Jane's bed. And that she'd had a good motive: she could choose between homelessness and John Cousins's death.

The evidence was circumstantial yet it became clear to the jury, as witness after witness took the stand, that Jane was well and truly guilty.

There was, for example, the testimony of the neighbour who had chanced upon Jane sawing the gap in the hedge. What possible reason could she have for engaging in such an unusual activity?

There was the odd exchange in the post office when Jane as good as protested to the postmistress that it wasn't she who'd been sending the insulting cards to Annie McGuire.

There was Jane's strange behaviour on the night when the Guards called to tell her of the incident. Her reaction had not been that of an innocent person.

Had the jury been allowed to see Jane's written – and highly incriminating – statement then they might have returned after ten minutes with a verdict of guilty. As it was they were gone for an hour. They found Jane guilty of murder but attached a rider recommending clemency on grounds of her gender and age. Clemency was indeed shown and Jane received a life sentence.

The judge refused leave to appeal, but it was nevertheless granted on 6 July 1933 in the Court of Criminal Appeal, before Chief Justice Kennedy. He too was loath to believe that Jane O'Brien hadn't meticulously and with malice aforethought planned and carried out a murder. He allowed the original sentence to stand.

Annie Hanly, the Roscommon Poisoner

The bride pushed open the door of her new home – and recoiled in shock. 'My God!' she cried. 'Do you expect me to live in this filthy hole? It isn't fit for a pig to live in!'

That was only the parlour, which looked as though it had never known soap and water. The filth in the kitchen was worse, but the bedroom was quite simply a health hazard. There were holes in the walls through which rats traipsed in and out with impunity.

Annie hadn't known what to expect when she married Phelim Hanly. In truth, her expectations weren't high – but this was too much for the thirty-four-year-old. She'd lived in the United States and had forgotten how primitive life in rural Roscommon could be.

Husband and wife quarrelled for three days and most of three nights. Annie refused to live in the house; she wanted the marriage to end there and then. Much of her ire was directed at her brother John. At one point she picked up a chair in the kitchen and told her husband she was going to break it over John's head. He had, after all, arranged the match. It was all his fault.

Annie's marriage to Phelim in 1933 was not unlike

many of the time. It was a union of convenience, more a business arrangement than a marriage – our modern word 'partner' would have acquired a rather different meaning if used to describe Annie's relationship with her husband.

Annie had worked hard in Boston, had cleaned and kept house for a succession of wealthy Irish-Americans. They paid her well and after ten years Annie had saved £700 – a small fortune in the early thirties. She could have saved more and bettered herself in the United States if her brother John, her sole living relative, hadn't written to say he was seriously ill. Annie packed her bags, drew her savings and returned to Strokestown, County Roscommon, with a view to taking care of him.

The arrangement suited both brother and sister. John had many friends in the town who visited at weekends. One such was Patrick Noone, a bachelor. He was a good-looking, friendly man of forty-six and Annie took to him right from the start. He would have made a fine husband were it not for the fact that Noone was almost penniless. He lived with two brothers and a sister on the farm the eldest boy had inherited. He had no prospects to speak of. John assured her she could do much better: he knew a man called Tom Hanly, who had a brother. . . .

Phelim Hanly was forty-four when Annie and he met at his brother's home. Hanly was no richer than Noone – but he did have a house with land attached. He seemed moreover a decent, hardworking sort of man and John convinced her that the pair would make 'a good match'. Annie believed him.

First, though, the finances had to be sorted out. On 16 January 1933 Annie met Hanly – again at his brother's house – and they arranged a marriage-settlement. Annie had money, Hanly had land; therefore she agreed to pay him £100 in his own name and another £100 into a joint account which they duly opened at the bank in Strokestown. All appeared to be well, they discussed their forthcoming wedding and Annie returned to her brother's house.

But that night she couldn't sleep, tossing and turning and brooding on her situation. She didn't love Hanly – in fact her feelings for him were negligible. Patrick Noone was the man she was attracted to, yet she knew there was no future there.

Next day she went to Hanly and told him the marriage was off. He was dumbfounded; this was the very last thing he expected. They argued; Annie demanded her money back. Hanly went to Annie's brother, who spoke to her. We do not know what he said but it was enough to convince her she was making a mistake. He may have reminded her that she was thirty-four and risked being 'left on the shelf'. To be sure, she could return to America but what would she do there? Continue skivvying for other women while growing older and more bitter? She could marry Patrick Noone but her £700 wasn't going to last forever. No, all things considered she could do worse than marry Hanly.

She gave in. The couple were wed on 18 February in St Paul's church, Strokestown. Annie's brother John gave the bride away; there was nobody else from her family present. The Hanlys, however, were exceedingly well represented; there were nearly sixty of them and Annie resented bitterly having to pay for their wedding breakfast out of her hard-earned savings. It was not an auspicious beginning to a marriage. Nor, indeed, was the prospect of spending the rest of her life in a vermin-infested house.

Phelim Hanly agreed that having rats strolling in and out of the bedroom was perhaps not the most salubrious of household arrangements. He boarded up the holes and even did his best to make the rest of the house habitable. Annie reconciled herself – as did so many women of her time and circumstance – to a loveless marriage. She shared a bed with Hanly, but only because she wanted children.

Time passed.

The signs that all was not well *chez* Hanly multiplied steadily. Annie's in-laws were a clannish lot who – with the possible exception of Phelim's sister Maisie – refused to accept her into the bosom of their family. For her part she detested them; hardly a day went by without a sister, brother, cousin, nephew or niece of Hanly's visiting and overstaying their welcome. They were moreover uncouth people, a far cry from the genteel folk Annie had grown accustomed to in Boston.

'I'm sorry to get mixed up with this rotten gang,' she said to friend and neighbour Anne Keaveney some five weeks after the wedding. 'As regards Phelim: I can't stick him.'

Nor did she have to stick him for too long more. On the night of 20 July, just five months after the wedding, a farmer called John Carr was passing the Hanly property and heard a woman screaming. He ran to the house and saw Annie and her friend Anne Keaveney in the doorway, the former in great distress.

'There's something wrong with Phelim!' she cried.

Carr went into the bedroom. Hanly was lying on his back in bed, his body arched at a strange angle. His eyes and mouth were open, he was lathered in sweat and his Adam's apple was unusually prominent. Carr felt for a pulse and found none. Annie joined him at the bedside. She appeared very distraught.

'Rub his hands, John,' she said. 'Rub his hands.'

'It's no use, Annie. He's dead.'

'He's not dead!' Annie insisted. 'He couldn't be dead.'

Carr assured her Hanly was indeed dead. He noticed that Annie wasn't weeping, despite her seeming distress. She left the house and went out onto the road. Five minutes later she returned, went to the bed and began to talk about Hanly in the most endearing and loving fashion. This surprised both Carr and Mrs Keaveney; Annie had never been heard to say a good word about her husband when he was alive.

There was no telephone in the house or anywhere else in the vicinity, and it was nearly an hour before the local doctor could be summoned. His name was Hanly and he pronounced his namesake dead, although he wasn't sure about the cause of death. He indicated that a post-mortem might have to be held.

This was the last thing Annie wanted – and told the doctor so in no uncertain terms. On no account did she want 'my husband's body cut up'.

Annie's version of events was straightforward when she spoke to the gardaí the following day. Two of them had called to the house: Superintendent Michael McKenna and Guard Willy Loftus. So far, it was simply a routine visit and no foul play was suspected. But they had to ask certain questions, they told Annie.

Superintendent McKenna wished to know about Phelim's movements on the fatal day. Annie told him her husband had been out haymaking since morning. At around five in the afternoon, when her own work was done, she'd brought him tea and helped him with the hay until both were tired out. That would have been about seven, she said. They returned to the house together.

'Were ye alone?' McKenna asked.

No, there was a neighbour there, Annie told him, repairing a hinge for Phelim. His name was Jerome Kennedy; her husband and he were old friends. It must have been about an hour later, she continued, when Phelim complained of a headache; indeed it had been bothering him all day, she recalled now. Annie knew just the remedy: a nice cup of tea.

All seemed well at nine o'clock, when Phelim rose and announced he was going to fetch some water from the river. Jerome Kennedy left as well, his repair job being done. Her husband was gone some fifteen minutes – an unusually long time; the river ran practically next to the property. He didn't look too well either when he reappeared; the headache had returned.

The couple said the rosary together. Phelim asked Annie to prepare his 'medicine'.

'What medicine was this?' McKenna asked.

'He'd stomach trouble,' Annie explained. 'He was getting medicine from Dr Hanly.'

The superintendent asked to see the medicine and Annie produced it. It was a compound containing cascara, an ingredient used as an intestinal tonic and as a laxative. Guard Loftus accepted the bottle, to examine later.

Superintendent McKenna asked her whether Phelim was present when she prepared his medicine. She said he was. She'd left the bottle on the table and gone to bed. Her husband joined her after a short time.

'Did you notice anything then?' McKenna asked.

'Not straight away,' Annie replied. 'But after about a

quarter of an hour poor Phelim said he felt he was going to faint. He was sitting up in bed. I went and got him a glass of water.'

The water didn't seem to do any good. Annie's husband was sweating heavily and was very pale. He told her to hurry round to his neighbour, Pat Keaveney, and ask him to come and help. Annie obliged. When they returned, Phelim's condition was worse. He had the appearance of a dying man.

Dying men need prayers said over them, and to this end Annie left the house again and elicited the help of Keaveney's wife Anne. Together the women prepared the ritual. Annie lit a blessed candle and placed it in her husband's left hand, exhorting Anne Keaveney to hold it steady. She took a crucifix from the bedroom wall and wrapped her husband's right hand around it. All three – the Keaveneys and Annie – knelt by the bedside and prayed.

An unusual thing, she told the Guards, was that her husband's mouth was wide open all the time. It was very unnatural. At a certain point he seemed to be trying to say something. Pat Keaveney had leaned close in order to understand the words. Hanly was asking Keaveney to go for a priest.

An hour later, just as farmer John Carr was passing by the house, Phelim Hanly was dead.

Superintendent McKenna was reasonably satisfied with Annie's story. The death had been sudden, it was true, yet such things happen. The Guards questioned the Keaveneys and they supported Annie's version of events. Dr Hanly, the GP, had been treating her husband for gastroenteritis. The bottle of tonic they'd taken from the house was a mild form of medicine. The doctor entered 'death from natural causes' on the certificate.

The funeral arrangements were made and the Hanly house prepared for the wake – but not before the rumour mill went into operation. Chief among the rumour-mongers was Jerome Kennedy, Phelim's friend. He'd known from the start of Annie's unhappiness with the marriage.

During the church service itself some of the whispered rumours reached Annie's ears. Kennedy, she learned from her neighbour Mary Neary, had been pressing Dr Hanly to seek an inquest and a post-mortem. The widow was livid with anger.

'They're accusing me of poisoning my husband!' she cried.

'Could Phelim have taken anything himself?' Neary asked. Annie shook her head vigorously.

The wake was an even more uncomfortable experience for Annie. When the guests thought she was out of earshot the rumours began to circulate again. She overheard her own brother John discussing the likelihood of an inquest and all this might entail. Annie grew angry once more.

'Why should there be a post-mortem?' she demanded. 'And why should his intestines be sent away?'

She turned to where Jerome Kennedy was sitting. He looked away.

'If there's anybody pushing enough to ask Dr Hanly for a certificate I'm sure he'll refuse to give it.' She caught Kennedy's eye. 'Only for you', she said accusingly, 'all this trouble wouldn't be.'

Yet Annie was also making trouble for herself: she simply couldn't keep her mouth shut. She spoke to Phelim's sister Maisie after the burial had taken place in the family plot in Strokestown cemetery.

'It's hard luck for me, Maisie,' she said. 'Phelim had no right to take me in like that.'

'What do you mean?'

'His debts! That's what I mean. He'd debts all over the place, and he never told me.'

Then she began to mumble something about poison. As far as Maisie could make out, Annie was saying that her brother couldn't have had poison in the house without her knowing about it. And, if he *had* got it, then it could only have been obtained from the medical hall in Elphin, and he would have had to sign for it.

These were mysterious words. But what really caused Maisie to become suspicious were the ones Annie uttered next.

'Oh, Maisie,' she wailed, 'why did I do it?'

The word was out in Strokestown and it soon permeated the walls of the garda barracks. Superintendent McKenna could no longer dismiss the ugly rumours. He approached Dr Hanly and demanded an inquest. Hanly acceded.

The State Pathologist, Dr John McGrath, was summoned from Dublin and Phelim's mortal remains disinterred. After a careful examination McGrath declared that the general organs were normal. The lungs, heart and liver were shrunken, but apart from that seemed healthy enough. Phelim hadn't died of any disease the pathologist could ascertain – yet he'd found one-sixth of a grain of strychnine in the stomach.

Suspicion fell on Annie.

The inquest was duly held and witnesses called. Annie insisted that Phelim and she had been on good terms throughout the five months of the marriage. Those who'd known the couple disagreed. A neighbour declared that, in his opinion, Annie regretted having married into the Hanly family. Members of the family backed him up.

Jerome Kennedy also concurred. He'd been present in the house when Annie had threatened to break a chair over her brother's head for having cajoled her into marrying Phelim and bringing her to 'that dirty hole'. According to Kennedy she'd often spoken of her husband as being 'thick'.

Yet if Annie had indeed murdered her husband then a stronger motive had to be present. It could have been an extramarital affair: one of the Hanlys testified to Annie having a 'liking' for Patrick Noone. But Noone gave the court to understand that Annie and he had never pursued their relationship in any way following her marriage to Phelim.

Superintendent McKenna thought he'd unearthed evidence of what might have been a motive: money.

His investigation had turned up an unusual aspect to the case. In January – a month before the wedding – Annie and Phelim had gone to the office of James Connell, a solicitor in Strokestown. The purpose of the visit was to have a marriage-settlement drawn up, making both joint tenants of the Hanly farm. On the death of one party the property would pass to the other.

But so would the debts, if there were any. The solicitor told McKenna that Annie had returned to his office at a later date. She didn't want the settlement taking effect, she told him, but offered no reason. McKenna recalled Annie's words to her sister-in-law Maisie: *'Phelim had no right to take me in like that. He'd debts all over the place, and he never told me.'*

Annie was arrested on 12 October on a charge of murder. Her trial began in the Central Criminal Court on 5 March 1934, with Mr Justice O'Byrne presiding. She pleaded not guilty, and both her counsel, Richard Hogan, and the prosecutor, Martin McGuire, knew it was going to be a lengthy process. The evidence was entirely circumstantial.

McGuire made much of Annie's reluctance to have a post-mortem performed on her husband's corpse. Superintendent McKenna backed him up. He stated that Annie had asked him repeatedly for the name of the person who'd suggested an autopsy. She also said: 'Should any poison be found, then for God's sake don't let the Guards come back about it.' It was an odd thing to say because before the inquest no mention had been made of poison.

The jury heard from Sergeant Joseph Diamond of Strokestown, the man who'd arrested Annie. 'What is this for?' she'd demanded of him. 'You know I didn't do it. I can't stand any trial today. I've no solicitor. Wasn't it brought out at the inquest I know nothing about it? You know I didn't murder him.'

Fair enough. Yet when Diamond was escorting Annie to the police station she turned to him in the car and asked: 'Did my husband die from strychnine poisoning?'

The sergeant told her he did.

'But he couldn't have,' Annie protested. 'There wasn't enough poison in him to kill a man.'

She appeared to have known this with certainty, it emerged. On 28 June 1933, less than a month before Phelim's death, Annie had visited the chemist's she'd spoken to Maisie Hanly about: the medical hall in Elphin, a town about six miles from her home. The owner, Mary Costello, could confirm for Superintendent McKenna that she'd sold Annie a bottle of medicine, made up from a prescription of Dr Hanly's. It was a tonic whose chief ingredient was cascara – but it also contained about one-eighth of a grain of strychnine. Had Annie known this at the time? Had Phelim?

Expert witnesses were called. Dr McGrath, who'd had the body exhumed, confirmed again that, in his opinion, Phelim had died of strychnine poisoning. He'd found one-sixth of a grain of the poison in the stomach.

But Annie's counsel, Richard Hogan, called his own expert: Dr JB Magennis, an eminent Dublin physician and an expert on poisons. In a lengthy speech from the witness box he informed the court that he'd made a special study of strychnine and its effects. He explained that the average fatal dose was between 1½ and 1¼ grains. In his experience, however, a dose as small as a half grain proved fatal.

This applied to strychnine (*nux vomica*) administered in its purest form. Magennis went on to describe the effects of strychnine when contained in cascara – the medicine prescribed for Phelim Hanly. And he concluded that the symptoms noted by Pat Keaveney at Phelim's deathbed were not consistent with strychnine poisoning. The customary spasms were absent, as was the intense physical pain. There was also the matter of the open mouth.

Annie's counsel asked Magennis what, in his opinion, had been the cause of death. Magennis considered that strychnine might have caused it – if Phelim had taken more than one-third of a grain. The problem was that the cascara bottle had contained only one-eighth of a grain, a harmless amount. On the other hand, strychnine might have killed him if he'd had a weak heart. Magennis had concluded that Phelim had not died of diphtheria.

'Would you conclude granular kidney disease as a cause of death?' Hogan asked.

'Yes,' Magennis replied.

This was all terribly confusing for those present in the court, not least for Justice O'Byrne himself.

'Dr Magennis,' he asked, 'if a man died from some of the diseases which you mentioned, do you not think it an extraordinary coincidence that his death should have occurred when there was a considerable quantity of strychnine in his body?'

'Yes,' the doctor replied – and launched into a detailed account of the effects of the poison on various individuals. The rate of solution, he said, was dependent on the person who took it.

'If taken in water, would it in that form be readily absorbed?' O'Byrne asked.

'It would. But not so rapidly as if mixed with cascara.'

'From the time a poison is taken into the body there is absorption?'

'Yes. And that goes on steadily until the moment of death.'

This last answer seemed to satisfy Justice O'Byrne. He then posed a highly pertinent question.

'Whatever may have been the cause of this man's death, it is highly probable that at some time during his life he took what may have been a fatal dose of strychnine?'

'Yes,' Magennis replied, and that concluded the evidence for the defence.

Hogan's case, on Annie's behalf, was that 'no poison was ever found on her' (a weak enough case in itself; she was hardly likely to carry it around in her handbag). He asked the jury whether they thought it was possible – if she knew enough about strychnine and how to apply it in the correct dosage – for her to administer the minimum to her husband, leave the house 'while her husband was still talking', and bring in her nearest neighbour, who could bear witness against her. Hogan repeated his claim that Annie had had no access to poison.

Unfortunately for Annie the prosecution had already summoned another neighbour who had a different story to tell. This was Jerome Kennedy, the man who may have been responsible for the inquest and subsequent trial. He'd been in the Hanly house on the fatal day and been present when Annie made tea for her husband, who was outside at the time. According to Kennedy, Annie had gone to a dresser in the kitchen, taken out what looked like 'a little crumpled paper parcel, like a paper containing a pinch of salt'. She'd then left the house to find Phelim, returned shortly and said, 'I don't see my *garsún*, wherever he is.'

Moreover the prosecution's evidence contradicted Dr Magennis's conclusion that Phelim hadn't died of strychnine poisoning. Dr McGrath, the State Pathologist, had stated that one of the symptoms of such poisoning is that the body becomes rigid. Pat Keaveney had told the court that when he tried to lift Phelim in the bed he was 'as stiff as a board'.

The prosecution urged the jury to side with McGrath and conclude that Phelim had died of strychnine poisoning. It was up to them to decide whether Phelim had administered it himself or whether Annie was responsible.

If the judge was confused by such conflicting evidence and opinions then the twelve members of the jury were even more so. On the sixth day of the trial they retired. After nearly three hours they returned, and the foreman announced that they couldn't agree as to whether Annie Hanly had murdered her husband.

Another jury produced a more definite result. When Annie was tried again the following July she was found guilty and sentenced to death. She appealed and the sentence was commuted to life. She died in prison and to the end maintained she was innocent.

Fanny Barber and the
Murder on Christmas Eve

Violence was no stranger to William Barber. At seventy-eight he was well into a quiet retirement, having had a full and chequered career with the Royal Irish Constabulary. Born in Sligo, he'd moved to Belfast at an early age, and had first-hand experience of the 1886 riots that left twenty-six people dead in the city, including four of Barber's colleagues.

He was assigned to the Central Police Office in 1895, where he shared control of the charge book. In his time there he recorded the arrests of some of Belfast's worst offenders, and often officiated in the Custody Court.

Yet William Barber was never directly involved in the arrest and incarceration of dangerous criminals. In fact, compared to those of other RIC officers, his was a fairly uneventful career. He failed to make promotion above the rank of sergeant and when he retired he didn't have an enemy in the world. At least, no enemy who could have wanted him dead.

Barber's wife died in 1907, two years before he retired from the force. They had two children, a boy who joined the merchant navy and a daughter who nursed at a Belfast hospital.

On his wife's death one of his nieces, Isabel Martin, came to live with him and look after the house.

He remarried in 1912. Fanny Malone, a Derrywoman, was thirty years his junior. Age, however, wasn't the only difference between them. Barber stood six foot three in his socks and was built like a stevedore. His bride was only four foot two; a petite woman, prematurely grey with a ruddy complexion. They were an unlikely couple. Barber's siblings and children whispered at the time of the wedding that Fanny married him for his money. This may have been the case, but let that question rest for the time being. . . .

Barber wished to make his retirement as pleasant as possible. He'd grown tired of the bustle of Belfast as well and decided to move to more peaceful surroundings. He found two adjacent properties for sale in the little village of Cultra on the southern shore of Belfast Lough. They overlooked the local yacht-club. One was a fine house, the other in a bad state of repair. Barber sold his home in Belfast and bought them both. Fanny and he moved to Cultra in 1921. Isabel Martin went with them.

Barber prized financial security above all else. To acquire extra income he rented out rooms to two lodgers, a Mrs Dornan from Downpatrick and a Mr Graham of Lisburn. Graham left in August 1933 but Mrs Dornan remained.

Fanny was as enterprising as her husband. She had the derelict house next door demolished and a bungalow built in its place. It could be leased at a good rate.

Barber also found himself a part-time job working as a rent collector for the firm of A & J Turner, property developers who owned some of the worst tenements in Belfast. The ex-policeman was a very suitable choice as rent collector: at times the work was so dangerous that it was necessary to carry a firearm in order to deter would-be robbers.

Barber had a firearm: his old service revolver.

On Christmas Eve 1933, Peter Conlon went to the kitchen door of his rented bungalow in Cultra, in response to loud and insistent knocking. There he found his next-door neighbour and landlady, Fanny Barber, in the company of Isabel Martin. Fanny was extremely agitated.

'Come over to my place at once!' she entreated Conlon. 'Something's happened.'

The other woman spoke with equal urgency. 'Please come quickly. Auntie is in terrible trouble.'

Conlon wanted to know what the matter was.

'Did you see a man prowling about the back of my house this evening?' Fanny asked.

He shook his head.

'You *didn't* see him? Well, didn't you hear him?'

Conlon admitted he had, on reflection, heard some noises that he couldn't explain. It would have been some time after eight o'clock, he remembered. There were two sounds, separated by about twenty minutes. The first resembled the noise of a picture falling off a wall – a wall in his own home. It had been accompanied by a light vibration. The second had come from a different direction. It had sounded like someone slamming a car door down by the boats moored at the yacht-club.

'There you are!' Fanny said. 'I knew you must have heard him. He was hiding in the garden all evening and I wanted the back-door kept locked.'

'Yes,' said Isabel Martin. 'I was away today and when

I came back I couldn't get in. Auntie had locked the front and back-door. She never locks both doors. I rang the bell and she called out to me from an upstairs window. She told me about a rough-looking man and that she had to lock herself in for fear of him.'

Conlon pulled on a jacket and went with the women to the house next door. It was a very short distance: the Barber house was only a few paces away. Fanny directed her neighbour towards the garage; there was a door at the rear that gave onto the back garden. Conlon wondered aloud why they hadn't used the front-door.

'My darling's lying in the hall,' was Fanny's enigmatic reply. She produced a flashlight and played its beam about the garage. 'Be careful!' she whispered. 'Maybe that scoundrel is hiding here yet.'

She opened the garage door and the two Barber dogs came bounding in from the garden to greet them, barking excitedly. Conlon knew the animals well; they never failed to bark when somebody called to the house. Fanny beckoned him towards the hall.

'Wait till you see my poor darling,' she said.

She shone the light. The front-door was barred from the inside. Ex-Sergeant William Barber was huddled in a sitting position against the timber, clearly dead. Conlon saw a wound below the right ear and another in the chest. Lying across the left forearm was a small five-shot revolver, its muzzle pointing at the dead man's palm.

'Mr Conlon,' Fanny wailed, 'who could have done that to my poor darling?'

If Conlon was shocked then Isabel Martin was doubly so. She screamed. He managed to catch her before she fell in a near-faint.

Conlon brought the two women back to his home and

telephoned for the police stationed in the nearby town of Holywood. Before they arrived he returned to the house next door accompanied by one of his Christmas visitors. He lit the gas lamp in the hall and examined the corpse. The hands, he noted, were still warm.

Conlon was a bright man and it suddenly occurred to him that he'd be questioned about the time he found the body. He looked at the hall clock; it was now 9.30.

Sergeant Patton and two constables were quickly on the scene, and they entered the Barber house as the trio had exited: by the back-door.

A doctor, Lawrence Donnan, arrived at the house some minutes later and examined the body. Barber, he declared, had been shot twice. The first bullet had been fired at such close range that the victim's left ear was seared and blackened by gunpowder. The projectile had entered Barber's neck under the earlobe, travelled downward towards the heart and severed the main artery. The second shot had been fired from some distance away; it had struck Barber in the chest at a downward angle and penetrated the heart.

Two bullets remained in the gun found on Barber's body; therefore three shots in all had been fired. Where was the third bullet? There was no sign of it in or near the place where the corpse had been found.

The police inspected the kitchen. There were no overt signs of a struggle; indeed this room, in keeping with the rest of the house, was as you might expect a country kitchen to be on 24 December. There were wreaths of holly and other decorations. The delightful aromas of Christmas baking still hung on the air.

A closer examination, however, revealed a gash in the middle bar of a chair. It had been caused by a bullet fired from the kitchen doorway leading to the hall. The police concluded that Barber had been sitting in the chair, and had risen before the assailant could strike again.

The bullet had ricocheted off the chair and struck the kitchen wall. The following day detectives would recover it from beneath a couch on the far side of the room.

Barber had been wounded by the first shot, the one fired at close range; drops of blood on the kitchen floor attested to this. He'd evidently made for the hall-door, attempting to escape, and the murderer had fired a third time.

But why did Barber's killer leave the revolver on his victim's corpse, as good as balancing on the left forearm? Was it a sign, a clue to his identity? Did he wish the police to know this? Sergeant Patton examined the body. In a pocket he found over £46 in notes and coins – a considerable sum of money for a man to be carrying about. There was also an expensive gold watch and chain. He ruled out robbery as a motive.

It was time to interview Barber's widow, who was being comforted in the rented bungalow next door. Patton spoke to her and took her statement.

Fanny told him that earlier that day there'd been four people in the Barber house: herself, her husband, Isabel Martin and Mrs Dornan, the lodger. They'd had their evening meal together in the dining-room. At about 8.20 Mrs Dornan announced she was leaving to catch the bus to her family home in Dundonald. William Barber offered to accompany her but Fanny wouldn't hear of it; he'd just recovered from a cold and she worried that the dampness of the evening might be bad for him. Isabel volunteered to go in his place. The Barbers retired to the warmth of the kitchen.

No sooner had the two women left the house than a man rushed in through the back-door. He was a stranger, wore a dirty grey suit, a tweed cap pulled down over his eyes and a brown muffler. He was 'squarely built and had a red moustache'. She thought him to be between forty and fifty years of age.

The intruder made a grab at Fanny but she eluded him, ran upstairs and locked herself in a bedroom.

'Was this man armed?' Patton wanted to know.

Fanny hadn't actually seen a weapon, but thought she remembered that the man had his right hand thrust in his pocket, as though gripping a concealed gun. Later she heard a struggle below and the sound of two shots. She fainted. When she came to, Isabel had returned and was ringing the front doorbell.

The sergeant placed a box on the table and opened it for Fanny's benefit. It contained the weapon found lying on Barber's forearm.

'Is this your husband's revolver?' he asked.

'I don't know. I know he does have a gun but I haven't seen it for some time.'

'Look at it again,' Patton persisted. 'Take your time. Now, is it your husband's gun?'

'Yes, I believe it is. He usually keeps it on top of a wardrobe in the bedroom.'

Next day – Christmas Day – District Inspector Lewis and County Inspector Regan visited the house to conduct a more thorough examination. No further clues to the mystery presented themselves. An inquest would have to be held.

But the following day the investigation took a surprise turn. Fanny Barber's doctor pronounced her insane and had her removed to the mental hospital in Downpatrick.

The insanity, it later transpired, was not a temporary condition brought on by her husband's violent death. All had not been well for some time in the Barber household.

Most Irish murders have been solved by diligent and, very often, inspired police work; the Barber case, on the other hand, owed its solution largely to the efforts of the prosecuting lawyers.

Granted, when the inquest was held the finger of guilt pointed unhesitatingly at Fanny – thanks largely to the work of Sergeant Patton. He'd gone over her version of events and decided it revealed too many discrepancies.

In the meantime Fanny had spent five months in the mental hospital in Downpatrick on account of 'nerves'. She was certified sane again and moved to a private nursing home in Belfast. It was there that she was arrested on 27 September 1934, brought before a special court convened at Holywood, and charged with her husband's murder. She said nothing.

Fanny was to be held in Armagh Gaol, pending trial. Her solicitor protested, quite understandably, that his client was still in a delicate state of health. Could she not be remanded in the nursing home? The judge refused. He did, however, make the concession that she be conveyed to the prison in a taxi rather than a police van. Fanny became hysterical as she was led away.

'I'm not going to Armagh!' she screamed.

But she did, and was kept there for eight days until her case was heard – again at a special court in Holywood.

The case against her centred on the impossibility of William Barber having committed suicide. The bullets that killed him had entered his body at an angle of forty-five degrees and, while the first had been fired at close range, the second had not. Also her story about an intruder was so far-fetched that few could believe it.

Yet if Fanny was guilty, as the prosecutor, Richard Carson, maintained, then a motive must be found. Carson already had a number of leads in this direction and he called Peter Conlon, Fanny's neighbour, to the witness box. Conlon repeated his account of the events following the murder. First Carson quizzed him about the mysterious intruder.

'Did Mrs Barber tell you about a man who had entered the house before her husband was shot?'

'No,' said Conlon.

This was another crucial point. Fanny had warned Isabel of a stranger 'lurking about' and given Sergeant Patton a very detailed description of the man who had attacked her husband – yet hadn't said a word to Conlon about the attack. Next Carson brought up the subject of the Barbers' marriage.

'Had you at any time a conversation with Mrs Barber regarding Mr Barber's age?'

'Yes.'

'How did it come about?'

'I made a comment on Mr Barber's continued good health,' Conlon said, 'and Mrs Barber replied: "I wonder will the old fool ever die."'

'And what was your response to that remark?'

'I turned the remark aside. I thought it was in bad taste.'

Carson made no further comment but called another witness: Isabel Martin, Barber's niece. It was found that her version of events tallied pretty well with Fanny's. But there *were* discrepancies, and Carson noted them. He asked the young woman to tell the court what happened when Fanny opened the back-door for her.

'She said there must have been a struggle in the hall,' Isabel began. 'She asked me to go with her there. She said she wanted me to see what had happened. But I refused to go.'

'Why did you do that?'

'I was feeling a bit giddy. I went back to the yard.'

'You didn't at that time know what had happened?' Carson wanted to know.

'I did not.'

'What happened then?'

'We went to Mr Conlon's house.'

'And you returned with him to the deceased's house?'

'Yes.'

'At what point did you learn of what had happened?'

'It wasn't until Sergeant Patton arrived.'

'How would you describe your uncle's condition on Christmas Eve?'

'He'd been in church that morning,' Isabel recalled. 'He was in good health and spirits when I left to go to the bus with Mrs Dornan.'

Then Carson changed tack. He wished to know about Isabel's uncle's financial situation. He asked her if Fanny had ever mentioned money in connection with Barber. Isabel remembered one occasion.

'I paid one premium on my uncle's life policy when my aunt asked me to,' she told the court. 'She was ill that day and couldn't go to town.'

'Did your aunt ever tell you about insuring her husband's life?'

'No, she did not.'

Carson knew this to be a lie. He had a statement from Isabel, taken by Sergeant Patton, that contradicted this.

He cautioned Isabel to this effect. She nodded.

'Did your aunt ever tell you as to whether or not her husband knew that she had insured his life?' he asked then.

'Anything that may be in the statement about her private affairs regarding the insurance is a mistake.'

'You say that in your statement,' Carson pointed out.

'My aunt told me that her husband wasn't aware that she had taken out policies on his life.'

So there was more than one.

'If I said it,' Isabel continued, flustered, 'it isn't true. I do not remember my aunt making such a statement to me.'

If Carson were seeking a motive for the killing then this could be it. William Barber was seventy-eight and not in the best of health; now it was emerging that his much-younger wife had taken out insurance policies on his life without his knowledge.

It would not be the first time such a situation had obtained.

There was another matter that still remain unresolved. Why had Fanny been brought to the mental hospital in Downpatrick hard on her husband's death? She hadn't gone there voluntarily but had been committed on the recommendation of a certain Dr Shane Magowan. Carson called him as a witness.

'Did the accused make any comment to you concerning her husband's age?' he asked.

'Yes. She said there was a difference in their ages which was causing trouble between them. She thought he might be doting.'

'I see. How did you find her own health?'

'Her general health was good – with the exception of her nerves.'

'Did you treat her for this complaint?'

'Yes. I gave her a tonic and a certificate as to the state of her health, which was as I have just stated.'

'For what purpose did she want a certificate?' This was a highly unusual request to make of your doctor.

'She stated that neighbours and people were inferring that she was insane and that was the reason she required a certificate.'

The plot was truly thickening.

'These people,' Carson continued; 'did she include her husband amongst them?'

'I do not remember,' Magowan replied.

'Is that all she said?'

'No.'

'Well, tell us!' Carson was growing impatient. It was like drawing wisdom teeth. 'Did you see her after that?'

'Yes. On December the twenty-sixth, nineteen thirty-three.'

'This would be two days after the death of her husband. What did you find then? Did you examine her?'

'Yes. I found that she was insane. I certified her and she was taken to Downpatrick Mental Hospital.'

The Winter Assizes sat in Derry city towards the close of 1935, and the Barber case was among the first to be heard by Mr Justice Brown. It was practically standing-room only in the court, for this was Fanny's home-town. Old friends, relatives, neighbours – as well as a great number of the morbidly curious – flocked to the court-house to learn the answer to the burning question: Is Fanny Barber insane?

Few doubted that she was guilty as charged, yet the evidence – so often the case where domestic violence or murder is concerned – was both flimsy and circumstantial. There were no eyewitnesses apart from Fanny.

Leading the prosecution was a man with a fearsome reputation in the courtroom: AB Babington, Member of Parliament and then Attorney-General for Northern Ireland. Within two years of Fanny's trial he was to ascend the bench himself and, another two years later, become Lord Chief Justice.

Having outlined the case for the prosecution, Babington homed in on the statement made by Isabel Martin. Part of it was flawed, he said. Isabel stated that she'd rung the bell because the front-door was locked. Fanny called out to her from an upstairs window, and asked her to use the back-door because 'a rough-looking man was going about the place'.

'This was a peculiar statement,' Babington told the jury. 'If there had been "a rough-looking man" about the place, a man who was evilly disposed and a danger to persons, would it be safer to come in by the back-door instead of the front?'

A fair point, you might think as a juror. The house in Cultra overlooked the main street and the yacht-club, where traffic was frequent. A genuine prowler would naturally choose to enter a house by the back-door.

But Fanny's defence counsel, William Lowry, failed to pick up on a salient matter. The Barbers kept two guard dogs in the back yard, dogs that never failed to bark loudly and excitedly whenever a person – known or unknown – approached. Isabel had lived in the house for years and the dogs knew her. Ergo: it would have been safer for her to use the back entrance.

Babington explained why Fanny instructed Isabel as she did. She knew that the corpse of her husband was propping up the front-door from the inside. She'd killed him and left him there.

And there could be no question of William Barber's having taken his own life. Fanny herself had ruled out this possibility. Barber had clearly been shot in the kitchen and had fled to the hall. The first bullet had entered his head *behind* the left ear. And, again, the angle of the entrance wounds ruled out suicide.

There was also, Babington continued, some trouble with time.

'So far as the Crown is able to ascertain,' he told the jury, 'there was no person in the house with the victim between eight-twenty and five past nine except his wife. I submit that the rough-looking man is a myth. Nothing can be more certain than that the hand that fired the shots which killed Mr Barber was the hand of his own wife. Do you believe that any human being would have remained in that house for upwards of twenty-five minutes without giving the alarm, without shouting out to some of the neighbours, without in some way attracting attention or endeavouring to go for assistance?'

It was a fine display of logic and it impressed the court. Babington had more evidence to hand.

'There were two dogs in the yard belonging to the Barbers,' he said, 'and, while these dogs usually barked at people calling at the house, they had not been heard that night.'

The Attorney-General next asked the jury to consider the remarks Fanny made to Peter Conlon, the neighbour. She'd asked him if he'd seen or heard a prowler. When in the garage she'd shone her flashlight around, suggesting that the intruder might still be in or near the house. Yet in her statement she'd claimed that the same intruder had shot her husband.

'Can you imagine an innocent woman,' he asked the jury, 'faced with this appalling situation, saying to Mr Conlon "Did you see a man prowling around the back of my house?" before they had gone to see the body or to ascertain whether the man was living or dead – or before anything was done for the wretched man who was lying behind the front-door with two bullet wounds in his body?'

Any killer worth his salt would hardly have hung around the scene of his crime, Babington said, but would have tried to put as much distance as possible between himself and the Barber house. He concluded that Fanny was thinking on her feet at the time, making up the story of the intruder as she went along. By the time she was questioned by the police sergeant she had a 'description' pat.

Then there was the niggling matter of the gun. Why should the killer have left it balanced on Barber's forearm? And how did he come by Barber's own gun in the first place? Fanny knew where her husband kept it: upstairs on top of a wardrobe. A stranger could scarcely have known this.

Fanny had also described a struggle; the police found no signs of one, either in the hall or the kitchen. Robbery wasn't a motive: neither Barber's money nor his watch had been taken. Babington concluded that Fanny's statements were 'so inconsistent and impossible in their various parts' that the jury would have no option but to come to the inescapable conclusion that her story was a complete fabrication. Fanny was as guilty as hell.

Babington called Isabel Martin, who repeated her version of events. As did Conlon. Babington sounded him out regarding the relationship between Fanny and her husband. Conlon cited again the remark Fanny had made about her husband being 'an old fool' and wondering if he'd ever die.

William Lowry, counsel for the defence, wasn't satisfied with this.

'How did you take that remark?' he asked.

'I took it more or less as a joke – and replied with a joke.'

Lowry wished to know how the pair got on together.

'They lived a happy life,' Conlon said.

'Did you ever hear them argue?' Lowry remembered that Conlon's bungalow was only eight feet away from the Barber home.

'Yes, but nothing more than any husband and wife did.'

Lowry produced the murder weapon as an exhibit; he then called Sergeant Patton and questioned him about the gun. If Fanny had used it, then surely her fingerprints must be on it.

But Patton told the judge that the gun had been tested for prints by Head Constable Brown. He'd found none because the surface of the handle was too rough.

'Might there have been marks on the smooth parts?' Lowry asked.

'There might have been.'

'Was the revolver handled by you with extreme care, considering its deadly importance?'

'Yes. It was put into a box.'

'How were you holding it when you were showing it to Mrs Barber?'

'By the butt. I took every precaution.'

'Did Mrs Barber handle the revolver? Did you make her take it in both hands?'

'That is not correct,' Patton protested. 'She did not handle it.'

'I suppose you know', Lowry said, 'that the ammunition should be examined for fingerprints?'

'It all depends on the class of ammunition. I don't believe fingerprints would go on these small bullets.'

'Not even when pushing a bullet in the chamber with the thumb?'

'I don't think so.'

'Could you have loaded the revolver without handling the barrel or the smooth portion?'

'Yes.'

Lowry passed the weapon to him. 'Well,' he said, 'put in an empty cartridge without handling the barrel or the smooth portion.'

Patton did as bidden. He stood up in the witness box and began to insert a round.

'Be sure it's an empty cartridge!' the judge cautioned and there was laughter from the public gallery.

'Had you done it before with the same meticulous care?' Lowry asked.

'Yes. But quicker.'

So Fanny's fingerprints weren't on the gun – but they didn't have to be. Sergeant Patton had demonstrated that, had she used the weapon, then she wouldn't necessarily have left prints. Lowry's ploy had failed. It was a setback for the defence but a worse one was to come. Babington called his next witness: Constable Kieren, one of the men who'd answered Conlon's summons on the night of the murder. He'd spoken to Fanny in her kitchen.

'What did she say to you?' Babington asked.

Kieren consulted his notebook.

'She said, "My dear has gone forever. Isn't it terrible, constable? I had a lovely home here."'

'Did she say anything else?'

The constable's next words were damning.

'Yes.' He read again. 'She said: "I have it hard. I always had it hard. All that troubled him was saving for one thing or another. He gave me an allowance and the remainder had to go for one thing or another. I couldn't get him to go for a week's holidays. He was afraid I would spend anything. See the shoes I'm wearing? I have them nine months, and I had to keep them rolled up in cloth for fear he'd see them."'

Lowry wasn't happy with this – and with good reason. He asked when the constable had written down this statement. Kieren admitted it was several hours later, when he returned to the station in Holywood.

But the damage had been done. A picture was beginning to emerge of the true nature of Fanny's life with her husband, and it was not a pretty one. Babington called yet another witness to reinforce the case: Constable Emo, who'd also accompanied Sergeant Patton to the house. His testimony was likewise revelatory. Emo read from his notebook.

'The accused said to me: "There's a plan of his family to do me out of the place."'

'The "place" being the house in Cultra?' Babington assisted.

'Yes. She said: "He has a son coming off the navy next year and a daughter a nurse. Neither of them liked me. All the furniture in the house belongs to my mother.

There is nothing in this house only what I made with my own hands and brought into it. I got that bungalow built last year as an income in case anything happened to him. He was an old scrounge. He never gave me anything only what barely kept the house. He always said he was putting it by for me, but I know who he was putting it by for. He made a will in favour of me, if I can prove there is nothing wrong with me."'

Here, then, was the reason why Fanny's sanity was so important. Her husband had accused her of being mentally unbalanced. Unless she could prove otherwise the house would go to his children. But Emo wasn't finished. He read out to the court Fanny's parting words to him.

'"Try and do all you can for me and get the sergeant to do all he can for me," she said. "They won't kill me, will they?"'

Barber's will was brought before the court's attention. Morris McKee, a solicitor engaged by Fanny, produced the original document. Barber had left everything to Fanny. McKee also produced several insurance policies on Barber's life, taken out by Fanny. They totalled £272.

Lowry dismissed the notion that Fanny would benefit financially from her husband's death. He pointed out that, besides the money Barber made from rent collecting, his pension was £82 a year. This, taken together with various investments, meant that the Barbers were very comfortably off.

As to the mysterious assailant, Lowry was convinced he really did exist. He believed the man to be a robber, somebody who'd known of Barber's work as rent collector – and who'd reckoned there would be money in the house on the day in question. It was a Sunday and Barber collected rents every Saturday, hence the presence of the large sum of money in his pocket.

But a robber is not necessarily a murderer and, realizing that he'd inadvertently killed Barber, he would have fled without taking anything.

It was time to hear Fanny's own account.

Once again her story contained inconsistencies. She spoke of the dinner party they'd had on Christmas Eve and how Mrs Dornan had left for her bus. At what time she couldn't say with certainty. Nor did she remember having dissuaded Barber from accompanying Mrs Dornan to the bus stop.

When the two women had left, Fanny and her husband went to listen to the church service on the kitchen radio, as was their habit. No sooner were they seated than the intruder entered. Fanny fled upstairs and bolted the bedroom door. On hearing two shots she fainted.

Fanny claimed that only ten minutes had elapsed between the women's departure and the intruder's entering the house. But Babington had noted the times given by other witnesses.

'Would you be surprised to know that you must have been unconscious for thirty-five minutes?' he asked.

'That might be so,' she conceded.

Babington questioned Fanny about her having been aware of a prowler earlier on. She hadn't seen him, she said, thereby contradicting an earlier statement. She'd simply 'heard noises' – and forgot when exactly she'd heard them.

'It has been suggested', said Babington, 'that this man may have followed your husband from Belfast.'

'It might be so,' she said.

Lowry had a new witness, one who seemed to support

the existence of the stranger. Her name was Elizabeth Richardson and she lived in Marino, halfway between Holywood and Cultra. She stated that on Christmas Eve a man had knocked on her door at around 8.30 in the evening and asked directions to 'the Barber house'. He thought it was 'opposite a farm'. Mrs Richardson didn't know the Barbers but had heard that people of that name lived beside the yacht-club in Cultra. She'd directed the stranger there.

Babington did his best to dismiss this new evidence. He asked her why she'd waited nine months before coming forward. She claimed she'd thought it was coincidence that the man had called, but later, on the advice of a friend, had approached Mrs Barber's solicitor about it.

Babington had also done his homework when news reached him of the new witness. He endeavoured to make Mrs Richardson's testimony appear as unreliable as possible.

'Isn't there another family of the name Barber between your house and the house of the accused?' he asked.

The witness didn't know.

'And isn't there a third family named Barber living at Marino?'

'I believe there was,' Mrs Richardson said, 'but I think they're gone now.'

'Weren't they there at the time?' Babington asked, knowing full well they were.

'I don't think so.'

'Isn't it true, Mrs Richardson, that you did not know what family of Barbers the man wanted to go to?'

'Yes.'

She was the final witness and the judge summed up the evidence. He pointed out that the evidence brought by

Babington fell far short of matching the certainty contained in his opening statement.

Babington disagreed. He maintained that his case was sound and reminded the jury of two important periods of time on the night of the murder. They were important to Fanny – whether innocent or guilty.

The first was from 8.30 to 9.05, during which time the crime had been committed. She was in the home for thirty-five minutes, either alone or with the assailant. If she were conscious then she must have known about the killing. She claimed to have been unconscious for a moment or two after she'd bolted the bedroom door until 9.05, when Isabel returned.

The second important period was when Fanny came into contact with Peter Conlon and others. She said she didn't remember statements she'd made to Conlon, and Conlon had submitted that these statements were inconsistent with her story.

'Thus she got rid of the two really important periods, the two most damning periods,' Babington told the jury, 'by saying she was unconscious throughout them.'

The jury had a difficult time of it. They could at any rate rule out suicide. But was the stranger a myth invented by Fanny? Barber had died by his own gun and only he and Fanny knew where it was kept.

Well, not quite. Barber used to bring the gun with him when collecting rents. He'd been murdered on a Sunday, therefore it wasn't inconceivable that it might still have been in the pocket of his overcoat – the collected rent money was still on his person. He might have gone for the gun, the intruder might have overpowered him and shot him with his own weapon.

The intruder could have followed him from Belfast.

Nor could the jury discount completely Mrs Richardson's evidence.

On the other hand the court had heard that all was not well between Fanny and her husband. He was stingy and didn't allow her to spend any money. The house and all she had would revert to Barber's children should she be certified insane.

The jury were unable to come to a verdict; both counsels had made their case admirably well. Fanny would have to be tried again.

The venue was different, this time Downpatrick, where the County Down spring assizes were held. But the players, with the exception of the judge, Lord Justice Andrews, were the same: AB Babington led the prosecution, William Lowry defended Fanny Barber.

A new jury heard the evidence from both sides. Babington laid emphasis on the fact that Fanny had told one story to the police, describing the intruder in detail and relating how he'd attacked first her, then her husband. How she'd escaped upstairs and heard shots before fainting.

Yet when Isabel arrived back at the house Fanny told her none of this. That couldn't be explained away. If the story about the intruder were true, Babington asked, why didn't Fanny tell her niece about it?

He continued, for an hour and fifteen minutes, to pick gaping holes in Fanny's testimony and the evidence produced thus far by her defence counsel. Apropos of the mythical assailant, did the jury not think he would have taken the weapon away with him instead of leaving it behind as evidence against him? There was moreover no motive for an unknown person to have murdered Barber.

Robbery could be safely ruled out. Revenge? Then surely the avenger would have come to Barber's home armed with his own weapon.

'When you look at the facts of her evidence,' Babington concluded his opening speech; 'when you consider the way in which the wounds were given; when you remember that the deceased was not robbed, and when you consider the fact that he was shot with his own revolver, and that no outcry of any description was raised, I think the probable conclusion is – and one which no twelve men would be reluctant to reach – that the man had been done to death by none other than the accused woman, who was the one person in the world about whom he would have no suspicion, and the one person whose duty it was to protect him from harm, and if he got into harm or trouble the very first person to go to his assistance.'

Once again Babington had shown what a fine orator he was. The following day, 11 March 1935, William Lowry came out of the traps in Fanny's defence.

'How could shots fired downwards have been loosed at Barber by his diminutive wife?' he asked. (Babington may have been napping at this point because when you think about it, the answer is fairly obvious: the first shot was fired at close range into the back of Barber's neck; he was seated on a chair twiddling the knob on the radio and Fanny shot him from a standing position; the second shot missed its target, hitting the back of the chair and ricocheting; the third shot – the fatal one – was loosed in the hall while Barber was lying against the door; his wife was again standing over him.)

Lowry spoke of the ferocity of the attack and asked the jury to accept that it could not have been the work of this little woman, a woman who'd lived on amicable terms with her husband for over twenty years – a man who'd made her the sole beneficiary of his estate.

Lowry went over the evidence he'd presented to the first jury, and added that not a spot of blood had been found on Fanny; her fingerprints were nowhere on the gun.

When called to the witness box, Fanny confirmed that she'd been 'on the very best terms' with Barber.

'Had you anything whatsoever to do with your husband's death?' Lowry asked.

'Nothing whatsoever.'

Babington then cross-examined her again at considerable length regarding her signed statement, the one she'd contradicted verbally. Fanny said she couldn't even remember making the statement, nor could she recall her conversations with the constables.

Lowry made a last attempt to save his client. In a dramatic show he had Sergeant Patton, who was about the same height as the deceased, stand beside his widow. The court saw that the top of Fanny's head barely reached the level of Patton's shoulder.

The jury retired. This time a verdict was reached. The judge turned to the foreman.

'Have you agreed to your verdict?' he asked.

'We have.'

'And you say that Fanny Barber is—'

But Fanny Barber collapsed in a dead faint before the judge could utter the final word. She must have sensed what it was going to be.

Isabel Martin screamed and had to escorted from the court, crying bitterly. In the meantime three female warders tried to bring Fanny round. They succeeded after ten minutes; Fanny began to howl and screech.

The court clerk attempted to persuade Lord Justice Andrews to have Fanny brought to the female witnesses' room but both counsels objected. She must hear the verdict in the courtroom.

A doctor was called to treat her and some time later Fanny was judged recovered enough to hear her sentence passed. It was to be death by hanging. Lowry wanted a stay of execution. It was not granted. She was scheduled to die on 5 April.

Fanny continued to scream and yell 'Leave me alone!' as two policemen restrained her. Many women in the courtroom were moved to tears. Some fainted. Babington and Lowry left in silence and Fanny was conveyed to Armagh Gaol.

But she appealed her sentence and won. It was commuted to life. She died in prison in 1952. Up to the last she protested her innocence.

Mary Agnes Daly and the Hammer Horror in the Church

Achurch is a house of prayer. Tradition dictates that a church is also a sanctuary, and history contains numerous accounts of men and women who sought refuge in churches when pursued by enemies. Soldiers respected God's house; even the forces of law were prohibited from defiling the sanctity of a church. It was a place of greater safety.

Mary Gibbons could hardly have thought otherwise when she pushed open the door of Our Lady of the Seven Dolours church, Botanic Avenue, Dublin. It was late afternoon on 10 August 1948 and Mary, a devout widow of eighty-three, was following her daily routine: dropping in to say a quiet prayer for loved ones both living and dead. At her time of life the latter far outnumbered the former.

She was the only person there as she knelt in a pew close to the altar. It was Tuesday and Gibbons was used to the weekday solitude of the building known affectionately as the Wooden Church; it has since made way for a more sober church, erected in the early sixties.

She was engrossed in her prayers a half hour later when she heard the front-door open and footsteps approach

~ 175 ~

slowly. Another weekday worshipper. Gibbons didn't even look round; her prayers took priority over her curiosity.

Without warning she was struck on the head by something hard and heavy. Her attacker was a young woman, slight of build, wielding a hammer. Gibbons recovered enough from the blow to be able to face the stranger. She received another blow and was about to be struck again when she managed to catch the woman's arms and hold them.

They struggled. Gibbons tore herself free and rushed screaming down the aisle, her attacker at her heels. The woman caught her again before she could reach the door. The hammer was brought down again and again on the hapless old lady. She screamed more loudly than ever.

The church door opened. Gibbons saw a man wearing a butcher's apron, stained with blood in places. She began screaming anew, thinking she'd stepped into a nightmare. But the butcher was on her side. Her mysterious assailant attempted to shut the heavy door by flinging her weight against it. The butcher was stronger; he forced the door open, grappled with the attacker and wrung the hammer from her grasp.

The butcher was joined by a second man and a boy. They stared open-mouthed at the two women lying on the marble floor, the elder bespattered with the blood that was flowing freely from her head.

'She attacked me,' Gibbons moaned.

But she was astonished when her assailant spoke for the first time.

'No,' the younger woman told the men, '*she* attacked *me*. She tried to take my bag.'

Sergeant Joe Turner didn't know what to make of the whole business. It was certainly one of the most unusual incidents he'd been summoned to investigate in a long time. He took the call at Whitehall garda station, Griffith Avenue, at a little after five, and was at the church within minutes.

The scene that greeted him was a grisly one. A small crowd had gathered around an old woman sitting on the steps, white-faced and bleeding from the head. A young man, a lorry driver, was cradling her in his arms, and he handed Turner a hammer. The elderly lady reached out a bloodied hand and gripped Turner's arm.

'Stay with me, please!' she implored. 'Don't go away.'

Turner produced his notebook. Old Mary Gibbons gave him an account of the assault. She pointed out another woman; she was being held by a man wearing a butcher's apron. He gave his name as James Canavan. The young woman he was restraining told him her name was Mary Agnes Daly. Turner took down *her* account of the incident.

'I was doing the Holy Hour,' she told the sergeant, 'and she was doing the stations. I heard her fumbling at my bag and on looking round saw her with my two bags and heading for the door.'

The old woman was shaking her head vigorously.

'I grabbed my bags and she held on and started to claw my hands,' Mary Daly continued. 'There was a hammer in the bag which I bought in Woolworth's a week ago. The old woman caught the hammer. I pulled it off her and gave her a wallop with it. I must have hit her on the head. I don't know where I hit her as I wanted to get away from her. I was afraid she was going to kill me.'

Turner did not know whom to believe. But the truth

could wait. At that moment old Mrs Gibbons needed medical treatment and he sent for an ambulance.

He inspected the scene of the incident. A trail of blood led from the steps of the church and up the aisle almost to the altar. It was a sickening sight.

The ambulance rushed Gibbons to the Mater Misericordiæ in nearby Eccles Street, where she was given emergency treatment. Her condition was critical: though her skull had not been fractured she'd sustained no fewer than fifteen wounds to the head. Her condition seems to have improved overnight, however, because she was able to give testimony the following day. A special court was held in the hospital ward. The victim, her head swathed in bandages and one eye severely discoloured, gave Mr Justice O'Flynn her version of events.

The attack, she stated, was totally unprovoked. The woman was a stranger to her – in fact, no doubt because she was still in shock, she couldn't be sure if Mary Daly had indeed been her attacker – and could think of no reason for the assault. She'd simply been saying her prayers.

'The accused has stated that you were interfering with some bags she had,' O'Flynn said. He read aloud a portion of Mary Daly's deposition: '"Is she saying anything about her taking my bags? I just struggled with her to get my bag back." Is there any truth in that statement?'

Gibbons denied this vehemently. She was the victim – and none in the court doubted this.

Mary Daly's solicitor applied for bail on compassionate grounds. Mary was a respectable lady, he told Justice O'Flynn, and it was hardly likely she'd attempt to flee the country. Moreover she had a baby and it would 'cause untold hardship if she was taken away from it now'. She couldn't afford to have the child looked after by another.

Not so, Inspector McCready countered: the child was being cared for by Mary's sister.

Justice O'Flynn appreciated the gravity of the case and indeed its unusual nature. The assault appeared to have been motiveless – a young woman attacking an elderly lady with a hammer, seemingly without provocation. He directed that Mary be remanded in custody and fixed the next hearing for the following Monday.

By Monday Mrs Gibbons's condition had improved somewhat. Nevertheless Mr Justice O'Flynn decided to amend the charge to one of causing grievous bodily harm with intent to murder, and remanded Mary for another week.

But before the seven days were up, old Mrs Gibbons was dead. Mary Agnes Daly now faced a murder charge.

Size matters, even to a jury whose brief is to weigh without prejudice the evidence presented by both parties. At the trial Mary Daly's defence counsel was at pains to point out that the twenty-seven-year-old was quite petite: barely five foot two. Gibbons, though advanced in years, had been very tall and well built. It was entirely possible that the older woman had been the attacker after all. On seeing the diminutive figure in the dock, those present in the Central Criminal Court on 10 November 1948 might have been tempted to believe that the deceased was indeed the guilty party.

The defence called an expert witness, Dr McGrath, who examined Mary's hands. He declared them to be 'small and rather weak'; in his opinion her right hand would have difficulty wielding a heavy hammer.

Mary's statement, made on the evening of her arrest, was read out in court. It seemed plausible enough. She'd been kneeling in the church and a big, elderly woman had been doing the Stations of the Cross. Mary heard a noise and looked round, to see the woman attempting to make off with her handbag and shopping bag.

I was mesmerized for the moment. I jumped up and grabbed her by the arm, and I said 'My handbag'. I thought she made a mistake.

She ignored me altogether and I thought she was deaf. The woman turned round and she either tried to hit me in the face or pull my hair. She did pull my hair. I then caught her round the wrist with my left hand. I shouted 'Help!' and the woman spat at me.

The shopping bag was then coming undone and the things in it were falling out as we were struggling around in circles. The woman seemed to be very strong.

There was a hammer in the bag which I bought in Woolworth's a week ago and the heavy end had fallen out at the end. The woman let the bag go and grabbed the hammer out of the bag. I was getting frightened. I thought she must be a madwoman. I called 'Help!' again as I thought she was going to fling the hammer at me.

I then caught the hammer and took it from her. She came at me as if she was going to scrape me or something. The woman's eyes were dilated. She was vicious-looking.

I struck her on the right arm with the hammer. She still seemed to come for me and my handbag was still on her left arm. We were then somewhere near the back seat and she screamed viciously. I gave her a blow of the hammer on the head as she was still clutching me. The blow put her off for a minute.

Then I tried to get out the door. I could not as the woman was leaning against it. I kept shouting for my husband and for help. I thought I heard footsteps outside, and someone tried to open the door from the outside. I gave the woman another blow of the hammer on the head. I did not mean to hit her on the head. I did not know where I was hitting her. I hit her to get rid of her. The woman then caught the hammer and she tried to pull it from me. I also pulled the hammer and I got her away from the door and we both fell to the floor.

The jurors' dilemma was self-evident: it was Mary's word against that of a dead woman. Gibbons had made a statement in her hospital bed, and it contradicted Mary's in almost every detail.

There were no witnesses to the actual assault. A nurse had visited the church briefly and could state only that she'd seen Mary there. Those who came later – they included a number of young girls – heard only the sounds of a struggle from inside. They couldn't enter as the two women were pushing against the door. They heard somebody crying for help and the words 'She's murdering me!' None could tell whom the voice belonged to.

The prosecuting barrister wasn't satisfied about the hammer – and who could blame him? It was a highly unusual object to have in your bag when going to a church to pray. He asked Mary if she always carried a hammer in her shopping bag.

'No,' she replied. 'That was the first time. I put the hammer in the bag that morning, just to get it out of the way.'

The prosecution had another explanation. Mary, the court was told, was in financial difficulties. She lived with her husband and young child in rented accommodation on Botanic Road. Kathleen Short, the landlady, testified that the Dalys were 'troublesome' tenants – they had a baby and Short wanted no children in the house. Moreover they were frequently falling behind with the rent – in fact such were the arrears that Short had served notice on the family to quit. Mary Daly later produced some of the rent but Short had refused it on the advice of her solicitor. She wanted the family out. A court order had directed that Mary should pay the rent and arrears at £3 10/- per week, due each Wednesday.

This sum was to prove significant. The assault took place on a Tuesday. On the Wednesday of the previous week, one of the priests at the Seven Dolours had given exactly £3 10/- to a woman he didn't know; she'd come to him in the sacristy begging for money.

It wasn't hard for the prosecution to make its case. Nobody brings a hammer into a church without good reason and the prosecution had a very good explanation: Mary was going to use it to break open one or more of the poor-boxes (a common offence in the 1940s when poverty was rife).

For some reason, the prosecution went on, Mary decided to rob the church's sole visitor instead. Mrs Gibbons was well dressed and Mary must have scented easy pickings.

Mary's defence was that Gibbons had attacked her with the hammer. Justice Davitt queried this.

'You are not a very strong woman,' he said, 'and you say that the old lady was very strong?'

'Yes.'

'Yet, notwithstanding the difference in strength, she received injuries from which she died and you have not a scratch on you. Do you wish to say anything about that?'

Mary did not – and probably with good reason. It seemed clear to all that her statement was a tissue of lies. The murder case was unusual in that it is rare for a jury to be presented with the victim's version of events; they had Mrs Gibbons's deathbed statement.

Justice Davitt directed the jury to bring in a verdict of murder and the jury obliged. Mary was sentenced to be hanged. She appealed and the sentence was commuted to life imprisonment. She served seven years in jail, and ten in a convent.

It was never discovered what might have driven Mary Agnes Daly to attack an elderly woman in such a brutal way, within the sanctuary of a church. She herself was a devout woman and made daily visits to the Seven Dolours. Although some wag remarked at the time that the initial letters of her name pointed to madness, the physicians who examined her pronounced her sane.

She claimed at her trial that on the morning of the attack she'd left the house with a purse containing more than £5. Somewhere between the church and the garda station in Whitehall the purse had gone missing. We have only her word for this.

It remains likely, then, that Mary Daly had the distinction of being the first woman in Ireland to murder another in order to acquire a week's rent.

Frances Cox, the Poisoner from County Laois

Poison has long been considered the instrument of choice of the woman bent on murder. We think of the notorious Lucrezia Borgia and shudder. Of the hundreds of poisons that can be administered to the unsuspecting victim, strychnine must rank among the most terrible of all.

It's an alkaloid, obtained from the seeds of *Strychnos nux-vomica*, a tree native to India which bears bright orange berries. Unlike many poisons, strychnine does not dissolve well in water or other liquids. Moreover it has a very bitter taste that's difficult to conceal; therefore great subtlety is needed when administering it.

The effects of strychnine are devastating. Once it enters the bloodstream it attacks the nervous system. The victim experiences a sense of suffocation, finding it hard to breathe. The sense of suffocation gives way to spasms and convulsions, particularly in the legs, making walking difficult.

Next the spine is attacked. The victim's muscles become stiff and rigid and the spine arches violently. The pain is intense and the spasm can last for up to two minutes. A period of relaxation follows each spasm as the muscle contractions subside. Then a new spasm kicks in, and the victim may experience up to five such excruciating contractions of the muscles before death by asphyxiation ensues. And all the time the pain is intolerable.

Death by strychnine poisoning is, in short, a fate you'd reserve for your worst enemy. Frances Cox evidently thought otherwise: she was found guilty of killing her own brother this way.

Richard Cox, a thirty-four-year-old farmer, suspected nothing when he sat down to dinner at five o'clock on Thursday, 26 May 1949. He shared the table with his widowed mother and sister Frances. They ran the farm together – a substantial property of about 125 acres close to Mountmellick, County Laois, and the foothills of the Slieve Bloom mountains.

It must have been apparent to Richard that some resentment was growing in Frances. She was a very able woman and capable of doing 'a man's work'; she did as much of the manual labour as her brother – and frequently more than that. Richard wasn't exactly a layabout but it was common knowledge in the district that he shirked his duties when it suited him.

At the same time Richard was devoted to his sister, who was four years younger. Their father had died in 1939, leaving the siblings to run the farm together; their mother took care of the house.

They were a close-knit family; when they were children Richard would always insist on accompanying his sister on her walk to school. He'd take her side, whether she was right or wrong, in any argument, and would refuse to hear a bad word said against her. All in all their relationship appeared to be a happy one.

But appearances, as we know, can be deceptive.

Richard finished his dinner that Thursday and pre-pared to leave. He'd an appointment with John Kelly, a neighbouring farmer who lived near Killeigh, some eight miles away. The day was warm and Richard decided to drink a glass of orange squash before setting off on his bicycle.

Halfway to the Kelly farm he suffered a sudden attack of cramps in his stomach. So severe was the pain that Richard fell off his bicycle and had to lie down in a field until the cramps subsided. He felt faint.

He was somewhat recovered when the local postman, Patrick Coulton, chanced by. He stopped on seeing Rich-ard, noticing a frightened look on his face. (This is con-sistent with the symptoms of strychnine poisoning; the victim, besides suffering great physical discomfort, will experience a feeling of dread.)

'Are you all right?' Coulton asked.

'I don't know,' Richard confessed. 'I've a sick stomach and a lightening in my head.'

Coulton was concerned by Richard's appearance. He looked very ill indeed. He helped the stricken man re-trieve his bicycle, then the pair continued to Kelly's farm on foot, Richard leaning on Coulton for support. The postman must have sensed at this time that Richard's con-dition was more serious than 'a sick stomach' because no fewer than five times Richard had to stop and vomit. Each time he did, he brought up blood.

His condition was a little better when he arrived at the Kelly farm. But John's wife Mary saw that his face was white; he was sweating and his hands were trembling. In fact they trembled so much that Richard could hardly hold the cup of tea she gave him and spilled most of it on the kitchen floor. He explained that he'd had 'a bad turn'.

Mary poured him another cup and this seemed to settle his stomach.

Indeed that great Irish panacea for all ills, a 'nice cup of tea', would once again be administered when Richard returned home at eleven that evening. His mother had gone to bed and only Frances was there to greet him. He related what had happened. Frances put the kettle on.

This time the tea didn't help much. Richard went to bed feeling sick and miserable. He got very little sleep, and tossed and turned for most of the night.

He felt slightly better the next morning but it was obvious to Mrs Cox that her son was unwell. Richard ate almost nothing at breakfast. The widow was not unduly alarmed by this for she knew that Richard did not enjoy good health. Occasionally, after a day's work, he would complain of pains in his heart and stomach. He took pills regularly for his stomach upsets, and the bottle was kept in a cupboard under the stairs, alongside medicines used for treating the livestock.

Richard should have stayed at home that Friday but he was a man who kept his word, and had promised two neighbours, the Weston brothers – William and James – that he'd help them that day to cut some sods of turf on the peat bog the two families shared.

His stomach was still queasy when he got back a little after eight in the evening; he could manage only bread and butter washed down with tea. He decided to retire early. He was still thirsty, though – perhaps from the day's work, perhaps from the dehydration caused by his vomiting. He asked Frances to bring him some more orange squash, drank it and went to bed.

No sooner had his head hit the pillow than Richard was seized by an attack far more violent than that of the previous day. His muscles contracted and his back arched in the tell-tale manner of the victim of strychnine poisoning; he couldn't move his legs; he was sweating. Richard felt he was dying.

Mrs Cox urged Frances to run to the house of a neighbour, Jim Fox, a good friend of Richard. Fox in turn hurried to fetch the local GP, James Keena. It was the first time Keena had treated Richard and he knew nothing of his medical history. On his arrival at the Coxes', Frances sketched briefly her brother's chronic 'fits' and heart complaints; she suggested to the doctor that the current trouble was probably 'more of the same'.

As yet, there was no suspicion that Richard's illness had been deliberately induced. Keena diagnosed neuritis, an inflammation of the nerves – a rather vague diagnosis in the circumstances – coupled with a heart disorder. Although he failed to make the correct diagnosis Keena nevertheless considered Richard's condition to be life-threatening. He was to be confined to bed, the doctor instructed Frances and the widow, and must not take solid food for at least a day.

Richard's condition had improved somewhat on the Saturday morning. It improved further when Frances obtained and administered the medication Dr Keena had prescribed: tablets and a liniment. Richard also decided to move downstairs to a bedroom adjoining the kitchen; he complained that the air in his own room was 'stuffy'. He managed to sleep for a couple of hours and was feeling better when Jim Fox called round to enquire after his health.

Mrs Cox decided to play doctor herself. She suggested to Frances that the patient should take 'a powder to help his bowels move' and thus prevent another attack. Frances was glad to assist; she returned from the kitchen with a little bottle of white powder, and some orange squash. Richard duly took the medicine; he complained that it tasted bitter, despite the sweetness of the squash.

Some minutes later, as Jim Fox looked on in dismay, Richard had yet another attack. His muscles contracted, he experienced great pain, and once more felt as if he was dying. Fox thought of summoning the doctor again, but the attack subsided almost as quickly as it had come. He urged the patient to try and get some sleep, and left the room.

The respite was short-lived. Just as Fox was going out the front-door, he heard his friend call out 'Jim, Jim!' Together with Richard's mother and sister he rushed back into the room to find the patient contorted in agony. His limbs were jerking like those of a marionette, his face was lathered in sweat.

Richard died in Jim Fox's arms before Keena could be called in. When the doctor came at last, he examined the dead man and declared that death was due to natural causes.

If Keena harboured no suspicions then he was the exception. Nasty rumours began to spread when news of Richard's death was made known. The Cox family was a prominent one in the district and – as is the case in all such rural communities – their business was known to all and sundry. It was common knowledge that Frances had plans to marry a local man, William Weston, a small farmer – one of the brothers whom Richard had helped to cut peat on the Friday before his death. Nothing unusual about that, save for the fact that the Cox family were Protestants, and Weston was Catholic.

William Weston lived alone with his mother on a six-acre farm adjoining the Cox property. No one knew for certain when Frances began 'seeing' him but it might have been early in 1948.

Undisputedly, Frances with her family wealth was a good 'prospect' for Weston, and marriage was discussed. But there was the problem of differing religions.

In 1908 the Catholic hierarchies in England and Ireland applied the papal decree of *Ne Temere*, a ruling that effectively drove a wedge between Catholics and members of other faiths. Baldly stated, it ordained that the Catholic religion should be the dominant one in the event of a mixed marriage. The non-Catholic, though under no real obligation to convert to the spouse's faith, was none the less obliged to have any child of the marriage baptized and brought up in the Roman faith.

William Weston was a staunch Catholic and a priest-fearing man. Frances and he discussed marriage; he persuaded her that theirs could take place only if she agreed to convert. Frances gave in. William spoke to the parish priest in Mountmellick, who arranged for her to attend classes in religious instruction. She dutifully did so for a time but soon grew tired of it – she wasn't particularly devout and found Catholic doctrine hard going.

Richard Cox, on the other hand, was a regular churchgoer. He strongly disapproved of his sister marrying out of the faith. But there was more. It was agreed that Frances should move in with Weston and his mother upon marriage and Richard was opposed to this. He enjoyed his sister's company; moreover he realized that Frances's departure meant his managing the farm alone, or hiring workers. Neither prospect appealed to him. His mother shared his dissatisfaction; she disliked the idea of her daughter marrying a Roman Catholic.

Frances, too, could not have been happy with the arrangement. Marriage to Weston would have meant a step down on the social ladder: she enjoyed running the Cox farm; the few acres of Weston's were no substitute. She wasn't prepared to give up the life she knew. One person stood in her way to complete ownership of the 125 acres: her brother Richard.

Superintendent George Lawlor was, by 1949, head of the Technical Bureau. Since his unravelling of the murder of Sonny Dan Walsh in Rosmuck two decades before, he'd acquitted himself brilliantly in many more investigations and had gained a formidable reputation as a detective. He knew nothing of the Coxes' affairs when he was called down from Dublin. He came at the request of the gardaí in Portlaoise, who had grave suspicions about the circumstances surrounding Richard's death.

As was the case with Sonny Dan Walsh the gossips had won the day. Richard was supposed to have been buried on the morning of 31 May. The hearse didn't make it to the cemetery; just as it was leaving the Coxes' farm, a body of Guards requested it to stop. They informed an outraged Mrs Cox that her son's body was to be subjected to a post-mortem examination.

It was performed that same evening; Richard Cox's remains were interred many hours later than planned. The corpse they buried was not intact, however; a number of internal organs were already on their way to Dublin, to the laboratory of the State Analyst.

Strychnine was found in the stomach – nearly two grains of it. For the poison to be fatal, a dose of between a quarter and a half grain is sufficient; the amount found in

Richard's organs could have killed a carthorse.

Superintendent Lawlor took statements from the three people who'd been present in the farmhouse at the time of Richard's demise: his mother, sister and Jim Fox. Fox referred to the bottle that had contained the white powder. He thought Frances had administered it but couldn't be certain – he was still traumatized by the sudden death of his friend.

Dr John McGrath, the State Pathologist, had concluded that strychnine was the killer. This being the case, there could very well be more of the substance present in the house, and Lawlor ordered a thorough search of the premises. Inside and outside, he said. The Guards went through every drawer in every cupboard of every room; not even chimneys were overlooked; the outhouses were searched, the rubbish tip gone over carefully.

They found no trace of strychnine.

In the 1940s the poison was relatively easy to come by. It was used by many farming folk to keep down rats and other vermin. Strychnine was freely available over the counter in all pharmacies.

The first lead came from the proprietor of the Offaly Pharmacy, Tullamore, who had a record of thirty grains of strychnine having been bought by Richard's late father in February 1936. It was a substantial quantity, and there was always the possibility that an unused portion might still be in existence, despite the intervening thirteen years.

Then one of the gardaí Lawlor had assigned to check the pharmacies in the area turned up a considerably more recent – and highly suspect – purchase. All chemists are obliged to keep a record of poisons and other dangerous substances sold. Nearer to the Cox farm, in Mountmellick, an assistant at the medical hall consulted the record and found that a Miss Frances Cox had bought thirty grains of strychnine – an identical amount to that bought by her father – in December 1947.

Ostensibly the purchase was for bona fide reasons: dogs had been worrying the Coxes' sheep and the poison was meant for them. Lawlor followed this up and found it to be true. The strychnine, the neighbours assured him, had worked: a number of stray dogs had been found poisoned to death on the 125 acres.

Frances told the police that some of her father's poison remained, and was kept in a tin in the cart-house. That being the case, why had she considered it necessary to buy more? And when she went with the police to look for the tin it was nowhere to be found.

Lawlor and his men searched the house a second time. Mysteriously, a bottle containing strychnine appeared on the floor of a lumber room off Richard's bedroom – where no bottle had been found during the initial search. It was close to the dead man's clothing, which had been examined by one of the detectives. Lawlor questioned Frances. Yes, she had been up in the room since; but no, she hadn't seen the bottle.

There was also the matter of Richard's suit; the Guards wished to examine it. After her brother's death Frances had stored it in the barn. She retrieved it, but the waistcoat was missing. It was eventually found – by Frances – stuffed behind a cupboard in the downstairs room where Richard died. Her story was that Mrs Dunne, the housekeeper, must have put it there when tidying the room. Mrs Dunne denied this.

The waistcoat was to prove pivotal in the investigation because traces of powder were found in the upper left pocket. The State Analyst declared it to be strychnine.

Frances couldn't have known this, yet when visiting the local shop the previous day she'd told the proprietor that the Guards had 'found strychnine in the pocket and that should convince them Richard took it himself'.

Frances was trying to persuade the authorities that her brother had committed suicide. It seems not to have occurred to her that taking strychnine is one of the most extreme methods of doing away with yourself. Anything from hanging to self-immolation is less protractedly agonizing. Had she suggested that Richard had accidentally taken a lethal dose of poison then all might have been well. And what reason did Richard have for killing himself? Frances couldn't produce one.

But she needed the theory of suicide to divert attention away from herself. Somebody had poisoned Richard; the poison had been administered over a period of time, and it was highly unlikely that the poisoner was a stranger. There were therefore only three suspects: Mrs Cox, Frances and Richard himself. Superintendent Lawlor was prepared to put money on Frances being the guilty party.

He produced the bottle of strychnine that had mysteriously appeared in the lumber room upstairs and examined it for fingerprints in her presence. Next he asked to look at her fingers. Having done so, he nodded sagely to the other detectives, giving Frances the impression that her fingerprints matched those on the bottle.

The trick worked. Frances suddenly remembered finding the bottle; it was the one her father had bought.

'On Saturday, 28 May,' she set down in a written statement, 'before my brother died, I was tidying the room upstairs where Richard was sick. It was about twelve noon and before Richard came downstairs I saw the same bottle that I had seen out in the tin in the cart-house two months before. I picked it up and threw it in the lumber room.'

She hadn't mentioned it to Richard, she said. But then she found a small whiskey bottle with something in it that resembled milk. She 'just got this idea into my head' that her brother might have been trying to poison himself with something diluted in the milk.

Superintendent Lawlor was having nothing of it. He knew Frances was grasping at straws to save herself. He also suspected why her murderous plan had gone awry.

His conclusion: Frances had set out to poison Richard and to make it look like suicide; therefore the poison had to be discovered in his room. But she hadn't reckoned on his wanting to move downstairs – or on Lawlor 'finding' her fingerprints on the bottle. She had to concoct the story of seeing the bottle in Richard's room and throwing it into the lumber room. Then, in order to show that Richard had poison within reach, she'd laced the pocket of his waistcoat with strychnine.

Lawlor took her into custody.

Six days were needed to try Frances Cox, beginning on 15 November. If the judge, jury and public were at first baffled as to the reason why this personable young woman chose to subject her equally personable brother to an excruciating death, the truth did not emerge at her trial – the law did not permit its disclosure.

It seems probable that the truth had been uncovered on 17 May 1949, nine days before Richard's death. The Laois gardaí were given a tip-off by an anonymous caller, who recommended that the Cox house be searched. The Guards discovered the corpse of a newborn child. Frances was arrested for concealing a birth.

Her trial was set for 22 July 1949. She pleaded guilty to the charge and was put on probation. But no sooner did she 'escape' punishment for one deed than she was confronted with another. Superintendent O'Sullivan of Portlaoise arrested Frances outside the courthouse and charged her with Richard's murder.

The concealed infant was not the first. The Portlaoise gardaí heard to their astonishment that Frances had been pregnant twice before – by whom we do not know. What became of the babies will likewise remain a mystery. Perhaps the Cox farmland contains their bones – and who knows how many tiny bodies lie buried in Irish soil, the children whose deaths were classified under the euphemism 'concealment of birth'?

But . . . if Frances concealed the births, how on earth did she manage to conceal the pregnancies? Neither she nor Richard went out much; neighbours could testify that they'd little or no social life. Yet Frances could hardly have kept her pregnancies secret from her mother and brother. She practically ran the farm and was therefore an active person – and you can't manage a farm while you're nine months pregnant.

I think it's reasonable to conclude that Richard was aware of all three births. He might have considered the third to be the last straw, and given Frances an ultimatum: Toe the line or clear out. Frances saw the lucrative farm and the status that went with it slipping through her fingers. Richard's death would solve this problem quite satisfactorily.

None of the above, however, was made known to the jurors who tried Frances for murder; the law forbade such disclosures. They learned only of Frances's marriage preparations – and an arrangement whereby she was to relinquish the Cox farm for the Westons' six acres, and to live moreover under another woman's roof. The prosecution attempted to present this as the motive for murder. Weston was cross-examined and admitted that a tentative marriage date had been fixed for June, the month after Richard's death.

Frances was put in the witness box and subjected to more than four hours of relentless questioning. She denied almost everything. She hadn't killed her brother; she hadn't asked the housekeeper to lie about the waistcoat; she denied telling Dr Keena that Richard suffered from epileptic fits. She maintained that her brother had committed suicide.

The prosecutor, Irving Forbes, wasn't buying this explanation and demolished it in his summing up to the jury.

'Would any man,' he asked them, 'having failed in such an attempt the first time, submit himself to the excruciating, tearing and writhing agony that Richard must have suffered on four successive occasions? Further than that, Richard's demeanour was not that of a man who was contemplating such an action.'

'Once you rule out suicide or accident,' Forbes pressed on, 'it was the accused who had the last and best opportunity to administer poison to the deceased. I submit that a dose was administered in a drink of orange squash, probably while the mother was upstairs. Not only had the accused that opportunity but she had another very important opportunity of washing up the cups, which she did.'

Then Forbes delivered the *coup de grâce*.

'In the matter of her own account of her conduct,' he

said, 'even before her brother's death, you have her evidence that her brother, whom she loved, had had this illness that he described on Thursday, and had the frightful, writhing agony, part of which she had herself seen on the Friday night. Yet when she saw a poison bottle in the room upstairs she said nothing to him or to anyone else about it, and did no more – if she is to believed – than throw it into a room nearby.'

The logic was impeccable, the arguments sound. Frances had had motive and opportunity. She was also the sole suspect and no amount of persuasion by her defence counsel was to deter the jury from returning a verdict of guilty. The public gallery was thronged and a crowd of more than a thousand awaited the verdict outside the court.

The judge sentenced a sobbing Frances to be hanged on 14 December 1949. She appealed but this was dismissed and a new date of execution set for 5 January 1950. She escaped the gallows, however – as did every woman convicted since of murder. Annie Walshe of Fedamore was the last to be executed, in 1925, in what is now the Republic of Ireland. Frances Cox's sentence was commuted to life imprisonment on 22 December 1949. Once again clemency had been extended to a member of the 'gentler sex'.

Gentler? It's not the word the Canadian writer Patricia Pearson would use. In her recent book, *When She Was Bad: Violent Women and the Myth of Innocence*, Pearson makes short work of the notion that women are less aggressive than men. Their aggression, she argues, simply manifests itself differently.

'Women tend to employ indirect strategies of aggression,' she believes. 'These are associated with ignoble traits like hysteria, duplicitousness [*sic*], manipulation, cunning. Unlike their male counterparts, women's aggressive strategies are not seen as brave or virtuous – they are by necessity underhanded. . . .'

Richard Cox, in his agonizing death-throes, might well have wished that his murderer had employed a more straightforward and less underhanded form of aggression.

That would have been kinder.

Mamie Cadden, the Blonde Midwife from Hell

At about five in the morning of 18 April 1956 a milk-float turned into Hume Street, Dublin. James Gleeson was making his usual delivery; his round included the Skin and Cancer Hospital.

He paused before climbing back into his van because he noticed something unusual across the street from the hospital. It looked like a bundle of dark clothing; it was lying on the pavement in front of the iron gate leading to the basement flat of number fifteen. The street was in gloom at that hour, illuminated as it was by weak street-lamps. Gleeson paid the bundle no more heed and left a few minutes later to continue his round.

At a little after six on the same morning, a rival milkman, Patrick Rigney of Lucan Dairies, was making a delivery in St Stephen's Green east. His round brought him past the entrance to Hume Street and, on glancing to his left, he saw a woman who seemed to be crouched over something beside the railings of one of the houses. She looked in Rigney's direction; she was dressed in a white coat and wore glasses.

Minutes later Rigney turned into Hume Street to continue his round. He spotted the bundle Gleeson had seen outside number fifteen. After a dull start the morning had turned out to be a bright one and, as Rigney drew closer, he saw two naked legs protruding from the bundle. The feet were inside the gateway to the basement flat. It was the body of a woman. She could have been unconscious; she could have been dead; he couldn't tell.

Intrigued – and not a little frightened – Rigney looked down the steps leading to the basement flat, where he assumed the woman lived. Another pair of eyes met his. There was somebody standing there in the shadows: a blonde-haired woman – not young – wearing glasses. Rigney recognized her as the person he'd seen earlier, standing over what he now knew to be more than a bundle of rags. The milkman jumped back onto his float and went to alert the gardaí. As luck would have it, a squad car was on patrol in nearby Merrion Row. Rigney flagged it down.

The officers followed him back to Hume Street. One of them went to the hospital across the way to seek medical assistance. No doctor was available at that hour, but a nurse was. Catherine Doyle joined the other Guard outside number fifteen and made a brief examination of the body.

The woman's skirt had ridden up to cover her head and this was in turn covered by a black overcoat. There was a nylon stocking tied loosely around her neck; a second stocking had been used to bind her legs, together with a pair of torn knickers. She was naked from the waist down and there were traces of blood on the clothing.

On the fifth step the Guards found a woman's handbag and beside it a small parcel. It contained personal belongings, including a pair of shoes.

There was a trail – of sorts – that led from the dead

woman's head and in the direction of a house two doors down: number seventeen. The head appeared to have swept part of the pavement clean as the body was dragged to where it now lay.

Nurse Doyle declared that the woman – she was aged about thirty-three – must have died some hours before. Rigor mortis had begun to set in yet the arms were still pliable. What intrigued Doyle was the strong smell of disinfectant. Its source was a dishcloth wrapped around the woman's legs.

More gardaí were summoned and the street cordoned off. Dr Maurice Hickey, the State Pathologist, arrived on the scene a little after eight and had the body removed to the morgue. In no time at all he deduced he was looking at evidence of a badly botched, attempted abortion. The foetus was still present and appeared to be about five months old.

Somebody had inserted either a syringe or tube into the womb for the purpose of introducing gas or liquid – the method of choice of certain back-street abortionists. The womb reeked of disinfectant – the same disinfectant that soaked the dishcloth found wrapped around the victim's legs.

It was clear to Hickey that the operation had been performed by somebody possessing a good working knowledge of such procedures; neither the uterus nor the cervix had been damaged in any way. Unfortunately the instrument used had perforated an artery and the resulting blood clot would have caused death within a couple of minutes.

Abortion was illegal. To cause a woman's death as a result of this illegal act was therefore murder in the eyes of the law.

Hume Street today is one of the most well-kept streets in Dublin's city centre. In 1956 it must have been particularly dirty because the trail of swept pavement leading from the victim's body wasn't hard to follow for Detective Superintendent George Lawlor.

Once again his name crops up in these pages: he was the gifted man who'd solved the mysteries surrounding the deaths of Sonny Dan Walsh and Richard Cox. Lawlor didn't lead the new investigation – ultimate responsibility went to Michael Wymes of the Central Detective Branch in Dublin Castle – but Lawlor played a crucial role.

There was little doubt in his mind that the trail began at number seventeen. This house was divided into flats. One such, at the rear of the first floor of the building, was rented to Marie Anne Cadden, a nurse. A postal worker lived on the floor above her. He'd left the house at about 5.40 that morning and paused to light a cigarette before walking in the direction of St Stephen's Green. Yet he does not appear to have seen the corpse – or, indeed, anything unusual.

Nor had Mary Farrelly seen anything out of the ordinary. But she'd heard something. She occupied two rooms on the first floor, and her bedroom looked out onto the street. She'd been woken at about 5.00 a.m. by sounds outside her door. It was, she said, as though somebody had been dragging furniture around. The noises lasted for about an hour and three-quarters. Farrelly noted that they'd paused at 5.45 – the time when the postal worker usually descended the stairs – and resumed when he'd left the house.

Two doors down the street, at number fifteen, a man who slept in a front room told the Guards that he'd heard what sounded like somebody sweeping outside early that morning. It was, he remembered, a continuous sound. And yes, it *could* have been the sound of something being dragged. . . . This could well relate to the trail that led from number seventeen.

The murder was, of course, the talk of that house. Nurse Marie Anne 'Mamie' Cadden and her fellow-tenant Mary Farrelly discussed the dreadful affair before the police came. Farrelly asked Mamie if she'd heard anything resembling furniture being lugged about. Mamie had not. She had, she told Farrelly, been 'fast asleep in my bed'.

Yet when questioned by Superintendent Lawlor the sixty-year-old nurse had a slightly different story to tell. She hadn't been asleep, on account of her arthritis. She'd had her radio on and that, presumably, was the reason she heard no noises. Mamie didn't know at the time that Mrs Farrelly had disclosed to Lawlor what Mamie had told her earlier – that she'd been fast asleep.

Then she said something she shouldn't have. The police had informed her they were dealing with a murder. Mamie responded with: 'It must have been a man who did that.'

This first interview took place in Mamie's room. Lawlor was quick to note an odd smell; it emanated from a bucket in a corner. It was the same odour of disinfectant he'd smelled coming from the corpse.

All things considered, Lawlor thought Mamie Cadden worth investigating. His colleagues had had dealings with her before. Moreover this was not the first time a corpse had been found in Hume Street: the fresh occurrence bore an uncanny resemblance to an earlier, unsolved, mystery.

The victim on that occasion was Edna Bird, a dancer in the Olympia Theatre, Dame Street. The post-mortem revealed that she'd bled to death as a result of a botched abortion. Rumour had it that the dying Edna had attempted to return to the abortionist to seek help. Rumour also had it that that abortionist was Mamie Cadden, a Pennsylvanian by birth, who'd lived in Dublin for many years. But nothing could be proven.

This time round, Superintendent Lawlor thought there was sufficient circumstantial evidence against Mamie to justify a search of her flat, and applied for a warrant.

In the meantime the new victim had been identified. Her name was Helen O'Reilly and her past was a colourful one. She'd been married to a man who'd functioned during the war as a minor Lord Haw-Haw, broadcasting Nazi propaganda under the name Pat O'Brien. He'd been arrested twice by the Irish authorities: once when he parachuted from a German plane into his native Clare. He escaped from Mountjoy and made his way home – only to be shopped by his own father, who evidently did not approve of his son's 'treason'.

The war ended and, soon after, O'Reilly and Helen married. They went to live in Clifden, County Galway, later moving to Dublin, where they ran a small hotel near Kingsbridge Station. It was not a success and the couple moved to County Wicklow. By this time Helen O'Reilly had given birth to six children.

Her husband left her and went to work in Nigeria as an electrician. The children were placed in homes and Helen moved in with her sister who lived in Preston, Lancashire. Garda inquiries revealed that she'd returned to Ireland on 4 April 1956, a fortnight before she died.

This last piece of information is intriguing in itself. The State Pathologist had decided that Helen was five months pregnant at the time of the abortion. Why had she returned to Ireland and sought out a back-street abortionist? There were more than enough of them in England in the 1950s. Helen O'Reilly, by choosing to have her pregnancy terminated in Dublin, was reversing a decades-old trend.

It will never be known how many unmarried mothers-to-be crossed to Britain on the Dún Laoghaire-Holyhead ferry in the years following the formation of the Republic up to the present day. Certainly there were thousands, and until such time that abortion becomes legal in Ireland – at the time of writing, a remote prospect – many thousands more will surely follow.

Helen O'Reilly could have had her pregnancy terminated by any one of a great number of back-street abortionists in Preston or another English city (abortion was still illegal in Britain). Yet she chose to return to Dublin. Not only that: an account of her movements during her last days makes strange reading.

She'd moved from flat to flat and stayed in a boarding house for a week. She spent two nights in a man's flat in Ely Place, just around the corner from Hume Street. Witnesses interviewed by the police spoke of her being unhappy and depressed. She was seen in Moore Street with a woman and a child. Could the child have been one of her own six who'd been left in the care of foster parents? She passed her evenings in various Dublin pubs, both north and south of the Liffey. She was last seen alive in Mooney's lounge in North Earl Street, at about 5.15 p.m. on the day of her death.

Lawlor and his investigating team had to link Helen O'Reilly to Mamie Cadden. Mamie acted as though she'd nothing to fear or to hide. Lawlor was to learn that this cockiness and arrogance were typical of Mamie.

'Search away,' she told him brusquely. 'You won't find anything here.'

She was mistaken. The detectives discovered a hatbox containing instruments that could have been used in an abortion: two duck-billed specula, forceps, syringes and rubber tubing. Mamie claimed that the box hadn't been opened in years – despite the presence of fresh fingerprints on the lid. The instruments, she said, dated from the time she'd run a nursing home in Rathmines.

This home had enjoyed a high degree of notoriety in the nineteen thirties. It could never be proven but the Guards felt certain that the institution was actually a front for an abortion clinic. Local wisdom had it that young women went there for terminations, and before long dead foetuses were found in the neighbourhood. Dead babies too. Yet the garda investigation couldn't pin a thing on Mamie Cadden.

There was also the occasion when she'd appeared in court in 1939, charged with abandoning a baby on a lonely road in County Meath. Mamie liked to drive round in a red sports car – a highly conspicuous vehicle in a time when the majority of motor-cars came in a choice of black, black or black. Eyewitnesses had spotted a blonde answering her description leaving a bundle on the road and roaring off in a red sports car. Wrapped in the bundle was a child, newly born to a girl who'd paid Mamie Cadden to have her infant 'adopted'. Dumping it on the roadside was Mamie's heartless solution. She, of course, pocketed all the money. Again there was no proof and the police were frustrated. God knows how many babies Mamie disposed of in this way.

Her reputation as an abortionist grew and she moved

to Upper Pembroke Street, a more up-market address. She did a roaring 'trade', partly through word-of-mouth recommendation, partly because of carefully 'encoded' advertisements which she placed in newspapers. A typical ad would announce Mamie's proficiency in the giving of 'hand massage and enemas'.

But she fell foul of the law in 1945 when she botched an abortion on a housemaid. The girl had to undergo an emergency life-saving operation in Holles Street hospital. She identified the abortionist and Mamie was sentenced to five years' penal servitude for the crime of 'unlawfully using an instrument with intent to procure the miscarriage of a woman'.

Mamie served her time yet didn't mend her ways. It *could* have been coincidence that the unfortunate dancer Helen Bird was found dead outside Mamie's new premises in Hume Street. No one believed it. But there was no evidence against her.

Now, more than a decade later, Superintendent Lawlor thought he had proof that Mamie Cadden was still up to her old tricks: the bucket containing the disinfectant.

Mamie gave an account of her movements the previous day. She'd gone to bed in the afternoon and slept until seven o'clock. She'd visited Mrs Farrelly for about twenty minutes, then gone to bed again. Somebody had rung her doorbell at about 10.30 – a man from Kilkenny, a former patient whom she'd been treating for baldness. She explained that this was how she made a living: besides treating baldness, she specialized in the alleviation of rheumatism, sciatica, constipation and other disorders. She returned to bed an hour later and slept until woken

by the sound of the post being delivered at eight o'clock
the following morning.

Lawlor wished to know more about Mamie's evening
caller. She claimed not to know his name – or, for that
matter, the names of *any* of her patients. But if the man
had come all the way from Kilkenny to see her, why did
Mamie keep him talking for an hour at the front-door?
No one could corroborate her story; indeed her fellow-
tenant Mrs Farrelly contradicted it.

The police took away the medical instruments for examination. They also took Mamie's diary and Lawlor
spent a week studying it. He returned to Hume Street to
ask the nurse to explain several entries. Sure enough,
Mamie seemed not to know her patients' names – she
referred to them, she said, by the colour of their coats. He
asked her to explain an entry for 17 April, the day before
Mrs O'Reilly's body was found. Different coloured inks
had been used and the original entry was obliterated.
Mamie explained that this had read '2 pm blue coats' and
referred to two women wearing blue coats who were due
to call but had failed to show. Lawlor was convinced the
entry had read not 'blue' but 'black' – the colour of the
coat found on the deceased.

And there was another reference to a black coat, dated
10 April: it belonged to a female patient whom Mamie
had charged £50, a very large sum of money for 'nursing'
services. Mamie had a ready explanation for this but
Lawlor saw that this entry had also been doctored.

He quizzed Mamie again about the medical instruments. She said she'd used them when practising mid-
wifery in her Rathmines nursing home. He asked her
again about her mysterious caller from Kilkenny. She
changed her story: the man had come two hundred miles

to see her, and she'd been treating him for rheumatism, not baldness as previously stated. And no, she wouldn't give his name, not wanting to have it 'dragged into the dirt'.

In the meantime a forensic examination of Mamie's flat and the hall outside it had yielded traces of blood. The fur of a cape taken from her room matched animal hairs found on the sole of one of the dead woman's shoes. More hair samples – human this time – found on Helen O'Reilly's coat, matched Mamie's blonde hair. Wool fibres on the same coat matched the material in Mamie's dressing gown. All the evidence pointed to the victim's having visited the flat at number seventeen.

Lawlor arrested the nurse on 27 May. The charge was murder. Though the intent was not to kill, the law held that, because Mamie had committed a felony – the performing of an illegal operation – she was guilty of Helen O'Reilly's death, regardless of intention.

It took ten days to try Mamie Cadden, beginning on 22 October 1956. She denied ever having known the victim, much less treating her as a patient, despite the forensic evidence to the contrary.

One aspect of her defence centred on her arthritis and this was (and perhaps still is) a bone of contention. That summer Mamie had been planning a trip to the Canary Islands in order to alleviate her ailment which, she insisted, was serious. So serious that she could hardly stand on the day Helen O'Reilly died, and had taken to her bed. She could, she said, produce medical authorities willing to testify in her defence. Yet when her counsel, Ernest Wood, approached a number of these doctors, all refused to examine her. Her bad name had preceded her.

It was, however, true that Mamie Cadden was a frail sixty-year-old, 'rheumatism' or no. The garda investigation had shown that considerable strength would have been needed to drag Helen O'Reilly's corpse from the flat, down a flight of stairs, down the steps of number seventeen, and to the place where it was found. Mamie could not have done it alone. But if somebody had helped her dispose of the body, then Mamie kept quiet about it and refused to implicate that person.

Wood was also hampered by Mamie's reputation. Inside and outside the court she was known to be an abortionist and the abandoner of *at least* one child. The jury, of course, weren't allowed to take any of this into consideration – but it was an uphill battle for any defence counsel. Wood's case relied on the prosecution's lack of hard evidence: it couldn't be proven that Mamie had ever met the dead woman. The evidence Lawlor and his team had collected was wholly circumstantial.

There was the bucket of disinfectant in Mamie's room and the strong-smelling cloth found bound round Helen O'Reilly's legs. But disinfectant is disinfectant, and that used by Mamie was freely available over the counter; any one of a thousand medical practitioners in Dublin would use it.

There were the hairs and fibres found on the corpse that seemed to match those in Mamie's clothing – the fur cape and dressing gown in particular. Again the prosecution couldn't make the case that fibres from these exactly matched those found on the body. The garments weren't specially made; they were off the peg; there were thousands more where they came from. The presence of the fibres might *suggest* that O'Reilly had been in Mamie's room, but you cannot convict on suggestion.

Then there were the hairs, the human ones: Mamie's on Helen's body and Helen's in Mamie's room. These days it would be easy enough to establish exact matches. The prosecution didn't have the benefit of DNA testing, only microscopes which suggested that the hairs were similar. Yet as if to highlight the impossibility of proving a true match, a pathologist carried out an unusual experiment on Mamie's behalf. He had somebody sweep the pavement of Hume Street between houses number ten and nineteen, and also collected hairs from a sweeping brush in the house in Ely Place where Helen O'Reilly had stayed for two or three days. The sweeping was done six months after the death – yet the samples found seemed to match those presented by the prosecution to 'prove' that the deceased had been in Mamie's room. The experiment made the prosecution's experts look like jackasses.

Wood applied to have the case withdrawn. The judge turned him down; there were still witnesses to be heard. The defence tried to discredit their evidence.

Wood cross-examined Rigney, the milkman who'd seen a woman standing over the body early in the morning. Rigney couldn't be certain it was Mamie, but she fitted the description well enough to convince the jury.

Wood tried to make much of the scarf tied around the victim's neck: it belonged neither to O'Reilly nor Mamie. There was also an umbrella found at the bottom of the steps leading to the basement of number fifteen. There was a fingerprint on it and it wasn't Mamie's. Wood tried to make the case that it belonged to the unknown abortionist who'd dumped the body near Mamie's flat. What better way to divert attention from oneself, he argued, than to leave the evidence of a botched abortion practically outside the premises of a known abortionist?

The prosecution, however, had the formidable body of evidence of the State Pathologist on its side. Dr Hickey was in the witness box for more than two days, during which time he gave his interpretation of the forceps, syringes and rubber tubing found by the police. He also used colour slides of forensic evidence for the jury's benefit. It was showmanship – but for a very real and serious purpose. Few in the courtroom could doubt that Mamie was the guilty party; after all, there were two dead women, two abortions in the same street, almost outside the same house. Coincidence could be stretched only so far.

The evidence may have been circumstantial yet it was compelling. The prosecution made the point that the coal cellars under number fifteen Hume Street would have made a good hiding place for Helen O'Reilly's corpse. Quite conceivably Mamie Cadden had been dragging it there when spotted by the milkman early in the morning. And why would a stranger lug a body to Hume Street and deposit it outside the door of a known abortionist?

'The jury may convict on purely circumstantial evidence,' Mr Justice McLoughlin said, 'but to do this they must be satisfied that not only were the circumstances consistent with the prisoner having committed the act but also the facts were such as to be inconsistent with any other rational conclusion.'

He then sent the jury away. They were back in less than an hour, with a verdict of guilty.

Such was the passion that Mamie Cadden aroused in the public at the time that there was scarcely a man or woman in the courtroom, outside the courtroom, or indeed sitting next to the radio, who did not rejoice when the judge pronounced sentence of death and fixed the date of execution for 21 November 1956. He concluded his sentencing with the prescribed words, '. . . and may the Lord have mercy on your soul'.

Mamie's reaction was odd. 'I'm not Catholic!' she shouted. 'Take that!' Perhaps she was trying to say she was an atheist and that the judge's 'Lord' was not hers.

She appealed and lost. But her solicitor managed to get her sentence commuted to one of life imprisonment. Hanging wasn't really on the cards. No woman had been hanged in decades. Mamie Cadden was fortunate that a new, more enlightened, ethos was making its presence felt in 1956.

Something happened to Mamie when in prison. We do not know what it was, because the records are lost. But she went insane and was transferred to Dundrum Central Criminal Lunatic Asylum in August 1958.

She died the following year: on 20 April. She might not have died peacefully, but she did die of natural causes. She outlived her final victim by a mere three years.

Noreen Winchester, the Patricide with Just Cause

The block of pensioners' flats is on Majestic Drive, just off Belfast's Sandy Row. Every capital has its Sandy Row: the inner-city housing estate where poverty and deprivation reign, and where violence – both public and domestic – has been so long a part of the societal landscape that it begins to resemble a normal way of life. Sandy Row has been called 'a dark and barbaric place'.

On Friday, 28 January 1993, one of the residents of Majestic Drive, a man in his late seventies, descended a flight of stairs at the side of the flats, intending to have his early-morning stroll. Something caused him to glance down. Between the stairs and wall he saw the body of a woman.

She must have been lying there for many hours and was quite dead. She'd been half stripped, beaten, raped, then strangled.

Two days later the body still remained unidentified and the Royal Ulster Constabulary appealed to the public for assistance. The brutal death had caused intense distress in a community that had seen, in a little over two decades, far more violence and death than was tolerable.

Rhonda Paisley, a city councillor for Sandy Row, spoke out against the murderer, and rapists in general.

'I have no doubt that the RUC will with vigour pursue the perpetrator of such heinous murder,' she said, 'but I regret that, if [he is] brought to judgement, his sentence will never reflect the total depravity of the crime.'

Ian Paisley's daughter was voicing the sentiments of a great many women in Belfast – and elsewhere in the island of Ireland. The law was seen to be too lenient by far where rape was concerned. But what the councillor didn't know at the time was that the murdered woman had once thought as Ms Paisley did: that the sexual abuse of women frequently goes unpunished. She also believed that it's sometimes necessary to take the law into your own hands.

There was a communal intake of breath when the identity of the murdered thirty-four-year-old, a mother of four, was revealed. She was Tina Wardlow, née Winchester, and Belfast remembered her well. By a cruel irony she'd met her death by a sexual attacker. In January 1993 she must have thought she'd left the horror of sexual abuse behind her. Sixteen years before, she'd sat in a Belfast courtroom and listened as her sister Noreen was sentenced to seven years in jail for the murder of their father.

Annie was only sixteen when she married Norman Winchester. She was also pregnant and that may have precipitated the wedding. Annie was the brightest and most outgoing of her family, one of many such working-class Protestant families who lived in East Belfast.

Her family had never had it easy. When she married Winchester she'd no rose-tinted visions of the future – but certainly nothing in her past could have prepared her for the ordeal that her marriage was to be.

Winchester was a good-looking young man, fond of socializing, gregarious, the life and soul of any party, with a fondness for the ladies. He liked nothing better than a night out in the pub, where he entertained his circle of cronies with his excellent singing voice. He was also known as a man who would 'stand his round' – shorthand for somebody who drank to excess in the company of equally thirsty friends. He liked to dress well too – no mean feat for a labourer who wasn't always certain of continual employment.

Winchester's socializing was to have a devastating effect on the family. Annie tried to keep a home together, but the home was never permanent as her husband and she moved from one mean housing estate to another. Some homes were more temporary than others: emergency accommodation provided by the social services when Winchester had drunk yet another week's rent.

The babies kept coming as well; there would be sixteen in all. Had Annie not tried home-made abortion preparations there would have been even more. And during her years of near-permanent pregnancy she managed to hold down a job as a stitcher in a clothing factory. The money she earned didn't go towards the upkeep of the home, however; Winchester pocketed it all.

The beatings started as soon as the honeymoon was over. At first they were for a 'reason': when, for example, Annie complained about Winchester's infidelity, or about his drinking and gambling. But before long the abuse had become part of Annie's life, and grew steadily worse and uglier in character. Winchester set out to humiliate her as much as he could, going so far as to rape her in front of the children.

She had few people to turn to; the neighbours refused to believe that Norman Winchester – kind, fun-loving, generous Norman – was an angel outside the home and a devil within. Her sister Nessie believed her, but Nessie had troubles of her own.

Then Winchester took a fancy to his daughter Noreen. She was eleven years old.

Incest is the final recourse of a certain type of coward and bully. When a depraved man has exhausted his brutality towards his wife, when the battering no longer gives him the sense of power he craves, when his wife has become numb to his extramarital flings, then he will turn on his own children. Some commentators argue that incest is an easy way out for a man determined to fornicate anyway. He's literally 'keeping it in the family'; no lace curtains in the street will twitch, there'll be no ugly rumours circulating in his local pub.

No one will ever know.

By the time Norman Winchester grew tired of beating and humiliating his wife, eight of their sixteen children had died, most in the first months of childhood. Noreen was the eldest, and it was to her Norman turned for his pleasures. It was Annie's final humiliation: her husband preferred her daughter to her. But at first Winchester concealed his unnatural acts from his wife.

We don't need much imagination to understand the horror Noreen suffered. Late at night, when all were sleeping, her father would steal into her room and rape her. Her silence was bought by threats of physical punishments – and Noreen, who'd seen the battering her mother endured, knew that these threats were very real.

As Winchester's lust – and bravado – grew, he sought

carnal knowledge with the child every time her mother was absent. He raped her in every room of the house, even in the kitchen. He not only raped her, he physically assaulted her too; he had to let her know who was boss.

Perhaps the most bizarre aspect of the incest was Winchester's habit of bringing his daughter for motorcycle jaunts into the countryside. Noreen knew what awaited her when they'd reached their destination. The wonder is that she didn't fall off the cycle from fear.

Eventually Annie discovered the truth. She was powerless to do anything about it. When she confronted Winchester he beat her senseless; when Noreen tried to come between her rowing parents she too was beaten. And not only by her father: the girl found herself the brunt of her mother's anger as well. We can only guess at the state of Annie's mind by this time – feelings of degradation and shame mingled with anger and jealousy.

In December 1974, when Noreen was seventeen, the situation became too much for Annie; the hurt inside her boiled over. By this time Winchester had been abusing his daughter on a regular basis for six years. And still nobody outside the little house in Suffolk, south Belfast, was aware of anything out of the ordinary. Winchester continued his extramural life as though he was an ordinary husband and father. Annie left home in desperation.

She wandered the streets of Belfast for several days. The police looked for her in vain. Eventually she was found by her sister Nessie.

Annie confessed all. Nessie was horrified, hardly daring to believe the things her sister had kept to herself for so long. Nessie urged her to file for divorce immediately and furthermore to seek the assistance of the social services. Annie followed her advice. The Housing Executive allocated her another home, in East Belfast.

Winchester discovered her whereabouts. He pleaded with her to drop the divorce proceedings – such a thing was a black mark against his reputation – and succeeded. He promised he would mend his ways, and Annie believed him. He gave her permission to take three of the children. Annie wanted Noreen to come and live with her but Norman refused to part with the girl. Seen in hindsight, we can take this refusal as evidence that Winchester had no intention of reforming.

We cannot imagine how Noreen must have taken the news that she was to remain with her brutal father while younger siblings were 'released' into her mother's care. Noreen would accompany her father to a new home in Hunter Street, Sandy Row, the street where he was born. She was to move there together with her sister Tina and three brothers. Annie, the mother, acquired a Housing Executive house in nearby Blythe Street, where she could look after the remaining three children. She could not have known she was condemning the other five to a hell on earth. As it was, she'd have no way of finding out: her husband forbade her ever to enter his new home.

From April 1975 until March 1976 Winchester held the five children in a grip of terror. They were virtual prisoners in the house in Hunter Street. The younger children were allowed out only to go to school and to help Noreen with the weekly shopping on Saturday afternoons – and every Sunday until 5 p.m. There was a dark motive behind the Sunday 'outing'. . . .

At first her father allowed Noreen to keep the job she had in a department store. The small wage she brought in went towards Winchester's socializing and the expensive clothing he was fond of. At the time of the move to Hunter Street he earned £45 a week as a scaffolder and Noreen's money was an extra 'perk'. Nevertheless he forced her to give up her job so she could take care of the other children. That was the pretext. In fact Winchester wished to cut all ties between the children and the outside world.

No one was allowed into 27 Hunter Street. The children had no friends and no one to confide in. No one outside the home knew that only £2 a week went to feed five hungry mouths; Winchester kept the rest for himself. He liked to eat well, was fond of 'a good feed', as they say in Belfast. Now you couldn't buy much for £2 in the mid-seventies. Noreen and the other four lived on a diet of spaghetti, potatoes and bread – and the leftovers from their father's own meals. This meagre diet wasn't enough to prevent malnutrition; the three boys learned to steal more food from the supermarkets.

Winchester seems to have approved of this last 'talent'. He was in the habit of sending the boys out on theft expeditions; he would sell or pawn the stolen goods.

But such petty lawlessness paled to nothing when set against what happened each Sunday, when Winchester ordered the four younger children out of the house. They were given strict instructions not to return before five in the afternoon. Winchester spent each Sunday repeatedly raping his daughter Noreen.

The neighbours in Hunter Street knew nothing of what went on in the Winchester house, that much is clear from newspaper interviews conducted later. One woman claimed to have often seen the children playing happily in the street. Another said she saw no evidence of malnutrition; the children always looked well-fed to her. They were 'kept clean and tidy and had their liberty'.

Noreen, yet another neighbour noted, 'kept herself very much to herself' but took the children to the baths every Saturday morning.

No one could believe that things were in any way out of the ordinary in number twenty-seven, that Norman Winchester's abuse was driving his eldest daughter to the brink. She had no one to turn to, no one who'd believe her. The stage had been set for murder.

It was the night of Saturday, 20 March 1976. Winchester came home drunk, had a quick snack and a beer from the fridge. He switched on the television and soon after fell asleep on the settee.

Noreen seized her chance. She knew that the next day would follow the now-familiar pattern: her father would send the younger children off to play in the park and she'd be subjected to yet another series of rapes and beatings. She described her anger as 'the flame that grew up inside me'. That night it became a conflagration.

Eighteen-year-old Noreen decided on the most drastic solution to her predicament: Winchester was to die. She fetched a breadknife from the kitchen and approached her father from behind. She plunged the knife into his neck. Winchester awoke with a scream and tried to rise. Noreen buried the knife in his back. She struck again and again – in total twenty-one times – until she was sure he was dead.

Stunned though they were by Noreen's action, her siblings knew that the body had to be disposed of, and quickly. It was unlikely that somebody might come to visit their home that night but they couldn't be sure. We do not know whether they helped Noreen pull on Winchester's jacket and shoes, but she more than likely had help when she carried the corpse out of the house and left it in a nearby alley.

It was found in the morning and the police were alerted. The conclusion of the constables? Winchester was the victim of yet another brutal sectarian killing – in 1976 such a murder was commonplace in Belfast.

The house in Hunter Street returned to a state resembling normality. With Winchester gone, Noreen and the others began the process of adjustment; their mother took them under her wing; they began to make friends. Months went by.

The RUC, however, remained unsatisfied about the sudden death. It could certainly have been the case that the IRA or a group of sympathizers had murdered Winchester, yet many aspects of the killing didn't jibe with the usual sectarian murder. Winchester hadn't been wearing his jacket at the time of his death – a fact easily deduced by the absence of knife entry wounds in the material – and he'd been drinking heavily. Why had he left the house in the first place? He didn't appear to have been killed on his way to an unknown destination. And no paramilitary group had claimed responsibility. The police began to turn their attention more and more towards the family.

The Winchester children broke under questioning and were arrested on 4 August 1976. Noreen and her sister Tina were remanded in custody; the boys were placed in separate welfare homes.

The trial, which began on 16 February 1977, was brief – and somewhat unorthodox. On the first day, Noreen was tried on the charge of murder, to which she pleaded not guilty. The jury heard the testimony of a variety of witnesses: the arresting officers, forensic experts, and Winchester's relatives. During that first day the truth about life at 27 Hunter Street did not emerge in court.

Then Noreen's defence counsel suggested to her that she plead guilty to manslaughter; they knew this would be acceptable to the prosecution. She agreed, although she claimed later that she wasn't fully sure what 'manslaughter' meant. She assumed that by choosing this plea her sentence would be lighter. The judge accordingly dismissed the jury and the trial took on a different aspect.

None of the adult members of the family – including Noreen's mother and her Aunt Nessie – gave evidence. It was left to her thirteen-year-old brother to tell some of the truth behind the killing.

The youngster obliged. He spoke in defence of his sister, explaining that the only time she was allowed out of the house was to do the weekly shopping on Saturday afternoons. He spoke of the starvation diet of spaghetti, bread, potatoes and their father's leftovers.

When it came to the killing he confessed all. He left no doubt in anyone's mind that Noreen was guilty as she had pleaded. But was it murder?

Manslaughter may be defined as the unlawful killing of a person without malicious intent and therefore without premeditation. A typical example is a death resulting from reckless driving. A slaying committed in the 'heat of the moment' also constitutes manslaughter. Lastly it is the absence of malice and premeditation that distinguishes manslaughter from murder.

On the face of it, Noreen's crime seems to have been premeditated. She killed her father on a Saturday night, in the knowledge that the following day was otherwise to bring yet another repeat of his monstrous behaviour.

The journalist Sarah Nelson wrote a moving account of the trial, published in *The Irish Times*. She drew attention to many anomalies, not least being the attitude of the Crown to the murder. 'No one began from the other end,' she wrote, 'and asked "why does a normal girl with no history of crime, aggression or disturbance suddenly act completely out of character?"'

The problem for the court, Nelson believed, was that it was a '*particularly bad case* of murder'.

> It was especially bad for three reasons. First, the killing was unprovoked: her father was asleep at the time. (In such cases, the concept of the slow-burning fuse has little or no standing, unlike the immediate situation. Thus drunken husbands who kill their wives in a violent argument have often received light sentences.)
>
> Secondly, the killing was premeditated. (This is a feature of attacks by women on men, especially violent men like Mr Winchester: women have virtually no chance in a stand-up fight.)
>
> Thirdly, the number of stab wounds (21), and the meticulous disposal of the body, suggested to them [the Crown prosecutors] callousness and brutality (even though the urge to clean up is normal in both victims and perpetrators of violence). It was this apparent cold-bloodedness which most disturbed one social worker. Deep down, she clearly felt Noreen's crime both wicked and unnatural.
>
> Even worse, Noreen was not even insane; a psychiatrist had proved this. Generally, in

the words of one barrister 'there was nothing
to suggest it was the way *a reasonable person
would have acted in the circumstances*'. It
was from this starting point that sense had to
be made of Noreen's crime.

And was it? Certainly her brother's testimony gave the
court pause for thought, as he outlined the circumstances
he and his siblings had lived in. It was a harrowing account and should have swayed the judge towards leniency. It did to some extent. Nevertheless she was sent to
prison – for seven years.

The decision must have been a tremendous shock to
Noreen, who had expected a very different outcome.
Indeed the entire trial had been completely at odds with
her expectations of justice. As she later said herself:
'Then in a flash the whole trial seemed to be over. Where
I was sitting I couldn't even hear X [the social worker]
and what was being discussed about me. . . . I had no idea
if seven years was hard or lenient for manslaughter.'

It was said at the time of her sentencing that Armagh
Jail would actually be *good* for Noreen: a psychologist
involved in her case seemed to think that prison would be
a distinct improvement on the dreadful home life she'd
been accustomed to, that prison might be a *liberating* experience for Noreen. Perhaps it was – anything was better
than the hell she'd endured as her father's sex slave.

Many, fortunately, did not share the opinion of the
psychologist, and were determined to appeal her case.

It began with a committee formed on 12 April 1978,
when Noreen Winchester had served fourteen months
of her seven-year sentence. The first step was to picket
City Hall in Belfast and collect signatures on a petition to

be delivered to Roy Mason, Secretary of State for Northern Ireland.

The 'Free Noreen Winchester' campaign was spearheaded by Women's Aid, the organization dedicated to the protection of and support for battered and abused women. As it gained momentum, other groups and individuals came on board, notably Oliver Napier, leader of the Alliance Party; the Northern Ireland Women's Right Movement, and the Association of Legal Aid Centres. The last was to play a key role in achieving an appeal hearing.

By rights Noreen should have been given the opportunity to appeal her sentence at the time of its pronouncement. She was not – and there is some controversy surrounding the matter. According to Noreen, nobody had asked her whether she wished to appeal, which seems unlikely. She told the press that she didn't even know what an appeal *was*. She found out eventually, from her fellow-inmates in Armagh.

While the campaign to free Noreen was hotting up, another was launched: Norman Winchester's relatives were determined that his killer remain behind bars. Winchester's brother Albert headed the counter-campaign, and was determined to clear the family name. He too organized a rally at City Hall. The first move was to involve the press: journalists from the Belfast *News Letter* accompanied him to Sandy Row, where they spoke to several of Winchester's neighbours.

A very different picture of the murder victim began to emerge. Winchester was, according to one neighbour, a decent family man. She'd often seen him 'coming home with one or two of the girls with bags of groceries – and I'm not telling you nonsense, because I know'.

He'd painted the house of another woman while she was on holiday. He was, she declared, a good man who perhaps 'liked a drink and a singsong but I can't believe he was the monster they've tried to make him out to be. He would have done anything to help.'

With the two campaigns running side by side, a hearing was held in the Northern Ireland Appeal Court and presided over by Sir Robert Lowry, the Lord Chief Justice. The case for the defence was that at the time of the killing 'there was an explosion in the girl's mind which made her lose all control'. Sir Robert listened carefully to the case set before him but ruled against the granting of an appeal. He said that the trial judge had been correct 'in principle' and that the sentence wasn't 'manifestly excessive'.

Yet all was not lost for Noreen. Sir Robert told the defence team that there was 'nothing to prevent the Government exercising the Royal Prerogative'. The ancient right of the English monarch to pardon a convicted criminal could be called upon.

It was up to Roy Mason, the Secretary of State. He returned to London and gave the case his 'full consideration', having carefully reviewed all the circumstances. In due course he submitted his recommendation for mercy to Buckingham Palace.

Noreen Winchester gained her freedom on a sunny April morning in 1978. She was twenty-one. The people who'd championed her cause spirited her away at once to a secret location in England. Noreen celebrated her release with champagne.

'I was in the sick bay on the night before I was set free,' she said to journalists. 'They came in, woke me up and told me that I was going to be out that day. I could hardly believe it. Only a few hours beforehand I'd been expecting to spend the next five years in prison.'

She was happy, she said, that the details of her prolonged suffering were out in the open. She also found it in her heart to forgive those who'd campaigned against her early release.

Albert Winchester's campaign to exonerate his brother was doomed from the start. Few could seriously believe that Noreen and her siblings – and their mother – had concocted the story of Winchester's years of brutality and violent incest. So profound was the stigma that attached itself to the family name that Noreen's younger sister Tina was only too glad to exchange it for another upon marriage.

And it was as Tina Wardlow that the thirty-four-year-old mother of four died at the hands of a depraved killer in February 1993, in Sandy Row, the district that had scarred her adolescence.

'During her life,' said William Moore, the minister who conducted her funeral service, 'she endured her fair share of trouble. Her life could have been described as tragic and her death could have been described as tragic.'

Few would disagree.

Susan Christie, the Beast
who Slew the Beauty

It was warm that March morning in 1991 when the Rice family went picnicking in Drumkeeragh Forest. The forest lies in the shadow of the peaks of Mona-hoora and Slieve Croob, County Down; here the river Lagan rises, before making a meandering detour past Lurgan and Lisburn, to empty at last into the sea at Belfast Lough.

Some hours later, Eileen Rice's two young sons alerted her to the woman who emerged from the woods and stumbled to the carpark. She had two dogs with her. She staggered a number of times and Mrs Rice feared she'd fall. She hurried to her.

The woman looked to be in her early twenties. She had light-brown hair, worn short, and was clad in a blue waxed coat, a grey sweatshirt and track-suit bottoms. The clothing, Mrs Rice saw with horror, was torn and stained with blood.

If she thought it odd that the woman should be wearing black leather gloves on such a warm day, she didn't dwell on the matter.

'Help Penny!' Susan Christie implored. 'Go and help Penny – please, please.' She spoke with an English accent.

While her husband and the boys looked on, Mrs Rice did her best to calm the hysterical young woman. She held her hands and tried to follow Susan's garbled words. There'd been an attack in the forest. A man was involved. And something terrible had happened to 'Penny'.

'Phone the RUC!' Mrs Rice shouted to her husband.

While he was gone Mrs Rice tried again to comfort the young woman. She was shaking uncontrollably and her speech was almost incoherent. The blood on her gloves was staining Mrs Rice's hands.

Susan Christie, despite the warmth of the early afternoon, was still trembling when Mr Rice returned. Helped by his wife he bundled her into his car and they drove to the home of Mrs Theresa Morgan, a friend in the nearby town of Ballynahinch. Mr Rice made a second call to the police, and Mrs Morgan summoned her GP, Dr Patrick McGrath.

The RUC arrived some ten minutes later, accompanied by an ambulance. Dr McGrath was already examining Susan Christie's injuries.

They were relatively minor. He found a small stab wound on her left thigh. There were a number of scratches and abrasions on her left side, and McGrath also noted 'some tenderness at the base of her skull and on one of her shoulders'. Her knickers had been ripped and were spattered with blood. McGrath observed that there was blood on Susan's gloves, and when she removed them he noted that her hands, too, were bloodstained.

McGrath concluded that Susan had been the victim of a violent assault. Yet he found it mildly puzzling that so much blood had managed to seep through a pair of expensive leather gloves. . . .

In a remote part of Drumkeeragh Forest two police constables came upon the corpse of an exceptionally pretty, blonde-haired woman. Her name was Penny McAllister. Her throat had been cut with such ferocity that the head was almost severed from the body. The instrument of death was found 260 yards away, evidently discarded by Penny's murderer. It was a knife of a type used by meat processors for boning sides of beef and large joints.

Joseph Carr of the Northern Ireland Forensic Science Laboratory examined the knife and ascertained that its owner had honed the five-inch blade to a razor-sharp edge. It was a fearsome weapon.

In Downe Hospital, Downpatrick, Susan Christie was describing the assault to the doctors and detectives. The attacker, she said, had struck Penny first. He'd then turned on Susan and tried to rape her at knife-point. He'd pulled down her trousers and slit her underwear. He'd stabbed her in the thigh and across the stomach. She'd fought with him, kneed him in the groin and escaped.

The RUC mounted a hunt for the killer. They made an aerial search of the area using a helicopter. Tracker dogs and officers combed the woodland. Four days went by and the police seemed no closer to capturing the man.

He should have been easily recognized – Susan Christie had provided an excellent description. She'd even drawn a picture of the man and the authorities had circulated a Photofit image based on the drawing. He was, she stated, 'of average height, about five foot nine and slightly built, with short, layered brown hair just above collar length. It was parted just off centre. He had blue eyes and seemed to have a bit of a stubble. He was dressed in jeans, white trainers and a green Barbour jacket.'

It was a description she'd repeat without deviation

during the next four days. Stronger still, her memory of her assailant seemed to improve with each fresh statement.

Susan was discharged from hospital on 28 March, the day after the murder. There were more questions to be asked of her, more statements taken.

The next day the investigating detectives decided that she was recovered enough to revisit the scene of the attack. They'd heard her version of events several times but wished to reconstruct the murder. Susan cooperated – though with some reluctance. She didn't know at the time that the police were beginning to doubt her story. They'd quizzed Dr McGrath on her injuries; McGrath had told them Susan could well have inflicted them herself. There was also the matter of the blood on her hands and on the gloves.

Two detectives and a woman constable escorted her to where Penny McAllister and she had entered Drumkeeragh Forest on the Wednesday morning with Susan's dogs.

How far had they walked?

'We did one circuit,' Susan said, 'and decided to go round once more because it was such a lovely sunny day. My shoelace came undone and I stopped to tie it. Penny went ahead with the dogs.'

Had she lost sight of Penny?

'Yes. The dogs had run on ahead. One of them was barking and Penny followed them. I rounded a corner of the path and saw Penny lying on the ground with a man standing over her.'

The detectives had brought her to the spot where the body had been found. Susan was greatly distressed but the officers pressed ahead with their questions. She was asked to go over her story yet again.

'I thought Penny had fallen,' she said, 'and that the man was trying to help her. I called out to Penny as I walked towards them. She didn't answer. As I got closer I saw blood and realized she'd been attacked.'

One of the officers was more insistent than the others. He wanted more details. How far exactly from Penny had the man been standing? Susan couldn't answer with certainty. She broke down in tears. But the detective persevered. What, he asked, had Susan done next?

'I was transfixed,' she said. 'I couldn't move. The man then turned and lunged at me, pushing me to the ground. I was fighting with him as he tried to rape me.'

The detective asked for more details.

'He began to pull down my tracksuit trousers,' Susan told him, 'ripping at my clothes. He was trying to stab me in the leg. He was hurting me. I could feel the knife going into my leg. It really hurt. He also cut me across my stomach as he tried to cut off my knickers. I was screaming for help. I started shouting "Daddy, Daddy, help me!", in the hope the man would think my father was coming and we weren't alone.'

What happened then?

'As I was screaming for help one of the dogs came running round the corner towards us, startling the man, who must have believed someone was approaching. I then kneed him in the balls and he let go and ran away. Then I went to help Penny.'

The insistent detective wished to know exactly how Penny McAllister was lying when Susan approached her. She told him again that blood had been gushing from Penny's throat. She'd attempted to stanch the flow by holding her gloved hands to the wound.

'I tried so hard to stop the bleeding. I shouldn't have left her there, alone. I was a coward. I just ran and ran.'

And she saw the attacker again? How far away had he run? Could she show them where exactly he'd run to?

Susan claimed she couldn't remember but led them to a place she thought she recognized. She pointed to a hillock. She'd seen the man standing there, she said, looking down at her.

'He just stared at me. I shall never forget those eyes for as long as I live. He then started to walk towards me and I just got up and ran for my life.'

She then showed them where she'd emerged from the forest. The carpark. It was a long way from the scene of the crime.

Susan's ordeal wasn't over yet. The police asked her to accompany them to Ballynahinch station, where she was questioned again and again. As the hours ticked by, her version of events became more and more inconsistent. The insistent detective was picking her story to pieces. Besides wanting further details of the murder, he wished to know more about Susan's friendship with Penny, wife of Duncan McAllister, a captain in the Royal Signals Regiment, stationed in Armagh.

The manhunt was on in earnest. The police had interviewed another witness – a man who claimed to have seen somebody answering the description of the suspect. He'd been seen driving away from the forest in a white Ford Escort XR2. Now the detectives had more than Susan's word to go on.

But they'd also interviewed her parents at their home in Lisburn. Susan lived there too, though she preferred the seclusion of her own room, and her parents respected her privacy. They never entered her room, and this was just as well. For more than a year, Susan and Penny Mc-Allister's husband had been using it as a love nest.

Duncan McAllister married Penny Squire in 1984. They made a remarkably handsome bridal couple: he the dashing lieutenant in red sash and black dress uniform, she a tall and beautiful eighteen-year-old with long fair hair and a perfect figure.

They'd met in Lippstadt, Germany. Penny's father was an educator for the Ministry of Defence and Duncan had a posting at the British Army base in nearby Soest. They fell in love and married two years later.

Penny had everything. She was exceptionally bright: she was reading at a very early age, took ten O-levels and passed them all. She was a gifted musician and had a clear soprano voice, which she used to great acclaim. At school in Germany she also revealed an acting talent and had the leading roles in school plays. It was taken as read that she'd go on to study at university. She would certainly have done so had marriage to Duncan not put paid to her studies.

But there was much to occupy the newly-weds in Germany. Duncan and Penny became enthusiastic skiers and subaqua divers. His career lent itself well to this second passion; the science degree he'd taken in the army led to his being sent on diving expeditions to many parts of the world. Penny would accompany him whenever possible.

Duncan received a posting to Northern Ireland in 1989. It might be thought that a young officer would have baulked at the prospect of being sent to this dangerous environment, where British service personnel were targets for terrorist attack. Not so. Both Penny and he were delighted. She'd tired of Germany, where they'd spent the first years of married life. Her husband wanted action.

The posting was in Armagh. Duncan was a signals officer with operational responsibilities. He worked hard and enthusiastically, yet missed his favourite recreation – the British Army had no diving club at the base. Duncan decided to form one and enlisted Penny's help.

The club was up and running in early 1990. One of the first to join was a twenty-one-year-old private in the Ulster Defence Regiment (since renamed the Royal Irish Regiment). Her name was Susan Christie.

She was a small, chubby woman – loud, brash and extrovert. She was in many ways different from Duncan's wife Penny. He hardly noticed her at first, but soon became aware of an 'asset' of hers his beautiful wife lacked: Susan had voluptuous breasts. She was in the habit of wearing tight-fitting blouses that showed them off to best advantage. Duncan was fond of big breasts.

Susan began her play for the handsome officer. During the lectures he gave to the diving club she'd sit gazing at him in frank admiration. She took every opportunity to be near him, especially when the club members retired to the bar. Susan contrived to become the life and soul of the party: talking, laughing and flirting with the men. Duncan found himself being drawn increasingly to her.

In July 1990 he let her know he wanted an affair. Yet he was at pains to point out to Susan that he saw it less as a long-term relationship and more as a sexual fling. It seemed to Duncan she was satisfied with this arrangement.

They made love in the open air towards the end of July. Duncan was surprised when Susan told him she was a virgin. But her lust made up for her lack of experience. Duncan was hooked.

During August and September the lovers found ample opportunity to be together, meeting twice a week. There were also the diving expeditions they engaged in at weekends. The problem here was that Penny invariably joined them – and Penny couldn't help but notice the attention Susan paid to her husband. She began to suspect that their relationship was other than platonic.

Then Penny became pregnant – despite using the pill – but miscarried. She hadn't told Duncan about the pregnancy, and now she didn't want him taking pity on her because she'd lost the baby. She wanted him to love her for her own sake.

By this time Penny was sure that Duncan and Susan were having an affair. She couldn't understand what it was that had attracted him to Susan in the first place. She wasn't pretty and Penny regarded her as a moody person who wasn't much fun to be around. She couldn't have known – or perhaps even have understood – that the affair, which had begun as something carnal, was developing into the most exciting thing in Duncan's life.

For nine months Susan and he contrived to have sex everywhere they could: in Susan's room in Lisburn, where once they were almost discovered by her father; in the back of Duncan's car; in the woods.

It should be remembered that both were army personnel serving in Northern Ireland. By making love out of doors they were exposing themselves to danger from three quarters: Penny might find out, the army might find out. So might the IRA. Out of uniform and without the protection of their fellow-soldiers they were easy targets for terrorist hit squads. Twice the lovers thought this the case, that their number was up. They were mistaken both times but resolved from then on to be more careful.

The turning point in the illicit relationship came in October 1990 when Duncan led his diving team – which included Penny and Susan – on a two-week expedition to the island of Ascension.

The fourteen days were tense ones for the trio. Each woman complained to Duncan that he was paying too much attention to the other. Susan's sulkiness and moodiness increased.

Yet she saw an erotic fantasy of hers become a reality: Duncan and she had sex under water, while the rest of the party – including Penny – remained on the surface, oblivious to what was taking place on the seabed.

The 'experiment' was a success, yet thereafter Susan's demeanour changed again for the worse. She refused to do her share of the work and was unfriendly towards everybody. It seems she was aware then that she could never have Duncan to herself.

Captain McAllister was being given insight into the true character of Susan Christie. Here was a woman who would go to any lengths to get her own way. She loved to flirt with men in order to draw maximum attention to herself, making crude remarks full of sexual innuendo. And woe betide the man who failed to respond. One such was a sergeant-major attached to her UDR battalion. Susan accused the man of sexual harassment. Her story was believed, and he was demoted. Another officer would say later: 'Susan Christie is nothing but trouble.'

On Ascension she changed again, almost overnight, and to Duncan's perplexity. She appeared now to want Penny as a friend. But Duncan was no fool. He'd seen often enough how Susan treated Penny: snubbed her, cut her dead when Penny spoke to her. Duncan sensed that this behaviour had caused Penny to grow suspicious.

Penny, on the other hand, had always treated Susan with respect and kindness. Indeed, she was a generous-hearted girl who never had a bad word to say about anybody.

Then Susan changed tack yet again, shortly before the expedition was wound up. She became intimate with Penny and sought out her company in favour of Duncan's. Once more she was the life and soul of the party.

The time came to leave Ascension. Penny was on a separate flight, with a civil airline; the army had refused to finance both the outbound and return flight of an officer's wife. The plane departed the same day as Duncan's but, once back in England, Penny had to make a detour to his parents' home to collect some belongings. She'd rejoin him in Northern Ireland two days later.

Susan spent a night with Duncan in his married quarters. It was there that he told her he intended putting the affair on hold. It was becoming too much for him. He needed a 'cooling-off period'.

Duncan saw little of Susan during the two weeks following their return to Northern Ireland. He was enjoying his cooling-off period when the phone rang on 2 November. It was Susan.

'I'm pregnant,' she announced.

They met three days later and Susan told him she'd decided to have an abortion. She burst into tears. Duncan comforted her, and advised her to give the matter more thought. Besides, the pregnancy had yet to be confirmed.

A fortnight passed. Susan told Duncan she'd seen a doctor who advised her to wait a further three weeks before terminating the pregnancy. At about this time Penny left for England to attend the twenty-first birthday party of her brother's girlfriend, leaving the lovers alone together for the first time since the trip to Ascension.

They made the most of her absence during that weekend – and their love affair resumed with more passion than ever. Further opportunity presented itself the following weekend: Duncan was scheduled to attend a diving conference in Portsmouth. He brought Susan with him. Their sex was 'electric'.

On 5 December, Duncan's office phone rang. It was Susan, calling from a hospital.

'I must see you, Duncan,' she said. 'I've had a miscarriage. I've lost my baby.'

She related what had happened. She'd been on night shift and begun to bleed heavily. She admitted herself into the hospital, where she was informed she'd lost the baby.

No one but he, she told Duncan, knew of her pregnancy – or of the miscarriage. So no more was said about it and Susan went back to work. Duncan was surprised she recuperated so quickly.

The love affair continued that winter in a haphazard way. Duncan and Susan saw each other less often than they'd have wished; making love in the back of a car on cold evenings was not to their taste.

Christmas brought two surprises for Duncan. Penny very nearly intercepted a card from Susan to him – one that was replete with evidence of their erotic adventures on Ascension. He destroyed it.

Then Penny announced she was having lunch with Susan. The news puzzled Duncan; he knew there was no love lost between the two women. He was in for another surprise. An angry Susan phoned him the next morning.

'You fucking bastard!' she raged. 'Why didn't you tell

me Penny has had a miscarriage?'

Duncan was thunderstruck. Were this true then Penny had concealed it from him. He was upset that his wife had been pregnant with his child and he'd known nothing about it. But he was also angry with Susan Christie. Her callousness and unfeeling attitude to Penny and him appalled him. He decided to make a clean break with her.

The army came to his assistance, in two ways. One: he received word he was to be promoted. He could choose between a staff job in Northern Ireland and a similar post in Germany. Two: Susan was leaving for England to train as an officer.

Susan Christie had always wanted a commission. Her father had served in the British Army when a young man; later he became a senior warrant officer in the UDR. He doted on Susan, and encouraged her to follow in his footsteps. His real ambition was that his beloved daughter would one day become an officer.

Susan had applied for training. First, though, she'd have to undergo pre-training at Beaconsfield, Buckinghamshire. She was notified that she'd been accepted; the course would begin on 1 April 1991.

Duncan saw himself being rid of the woman who was fast becoming a dangerous nuisance. He knew it was only a matter of time before the affair was out in the open. He couldn't risk it. It might mean the end of his marriage and the ruination of his career.

Susan was devastated to learn that Duncan and Penny had booked a skiing holiday in Germany in February. She'd been looking forward so much to spending Valentine's Day with him. Moreover it left them only three more weeks together following Duncan's return. She told

Duncan how much she loved him.

This was upsetting. Duncan was very fond of Susan but his love was reserved for his wife. As things turned out, the McAllisters enjoyed what amounted to a second honeymoon. They both loved skiing and the romantic evenings that went with it. That holiday was to bring them closer than they'd been in years.

Time was running out for Susan, and she knew it. When the McAllisters came home she tried many ruses to see Duncan – going so far as dropping by to invite him and Penny to a screening of the children's film *Teenage Mutant Ninja Turtles*. There were, understandably, no takers and Susan went away in a huff.

More ominously, Susan invited Penny to dive with her. Penny's aversion to diving in the cold, dark water off Northern Ireland was well known. Equally well known was Susan's strong dislike of Penny. As her friend Annette later suggested, it's very easy for a person to kill another under water – and extremely hard to prove that such a death was not accidental.

Duncan became suspicious and collared Susan about it.

'I just thought it would be nice to dive with Penny before I go on my course,' she explained. 'I might never get the chance again.'

'But', said Duncan, 'you've never wanted to dive with her before and would go mad if I even suggested it.'

'I've changed my mind. I get on better with her now.'

This wasn't strictly true and Duncan knew it. Minutes later Susan told him of her doubts about wanting to proceed with her officer training. He knew what this really meant: Susan wasn't prepared to end their affair just yet. He encouraged her to go for the commission.

The dive went ahead but Penny stayed out of the water. Susan's friend Annette joined her instead.

The following weekend was to be the last Duncan and Susan would spend together as lovers. Penny left for Dublin with a number of other army wives and Susan moved into Duncan's married quarters. Their lovemaking was intense – by times tender, by other times torrid. Susan knew she was losing the man she loved.

'I'd like to come back at weekends,' she said, 'to dive, and see you and the others.'

'That's great. But you do realize it would have to be on a platonic basis.'

'But why?'

'Because I would be with Penny.'

'Do you love me?' Susan asked.

'Yes, I do, and always will. I'd like to think we could always remain friends.'

These were not the words Susan wished to hear. They were as a red rag to a bull. Nine days later Penny McAllister would lie dead in a remote quarter of a forest, murdered by a woman who wanted more than platonic love.

Crown Prosecutor John Creaney stood in the courtroom in Downpatrick on 1 June 1992, and told the jury why Duncan McAllister's wife had to die. Penny was 'an obstacle', he said, and Susan Christie was 'determined to remove that obstacle'.

Susan's plea was that of manslaughter. Creaney insisted that Penny's killing was meticulously planned murder in the first degree.

The evidence was compelling. A week before the fatal stabbing in Drumkeeragh Forest, Penny had phoned her lover to tell him about a new place she'd found to walk the dogs – both her own and the McAllisters'. They'd love it. So would Penny, she said, and she'd arranged a walk there that coming Monday. As it turned out, Susan postponed the outing until the Wednesday. She'd taken considerable pains to reconnoitre the place and had lured Penny there.

She had, Creaney told the jury, 'gone to the extent of making sure they were in a part that was lonely, before she launched her attack with this knife upon her unsuspecting victim from behind.' She'd then stabbed and cut herself, and ripped her clothing, in order to convince the police that both women had been attacked by a third party.

Susan's story had not held up under police questioning; three days after the killing she'd finally given in. She did not, however, confess to having murdered Penny. She claimed, over and over, that she remembered nothing of the attack in the forest.

Susan's interrogators were unconvinced. This was due in part to Duncan: he had admitted to the affair. This admission had pointed to a motive: jilted mistress murders wife; 'obstacle' is removed.

The police knew many intimate details concerning the affair; Susan had divulged them willingly. Much of what she'd said was the truth. She did, however, allege that Penny was aware of what was going on – and had, indeed, condoned it. The McAllisters' marriage, Susan claimed, had been an 'open' one. She even went so far as to accuse the unfortunate Penny of having taken many lovers herself.

This was a downright and scurrilous lie.

It wasn't long before the police exposed the story of the mysterious attacker as a complete fabrication. The hunt was called off, Susan Christie was charged with Penny's murder and remanded in Lisburn to await trial.

The trial was presided over by Lord Justice Kelly. From the first day on he displayed an unusual degree of compassion for the woman in the dock. When expert witnesses described the nature of Penny McAllister's injuries in horrific detail – and horrific the injuries were – Susan would break down and Kelly would suspend the hearing for her benefit.

Duncan gave evidence during two days of the trial. He did not acquit himself well either as husband or extramarital lover. When questioned about Susan's pregnancy he denied three times that he had suggested abortion, yet finally admitted that he had, after all, stated to the police that he'd given her three options, including termination.

He also replied to questions that concerned the differences in rank and class between Susan and him. She was a private, the daughter of a non-commissioned officer, and army regulations forbade them even meeting socially, let alone conducting an affair. (At the time of this book going to press, a new code proposed by the Ministry of Defence and approved by the British Army permits carnal knowledge between officers and lower ranks, including adultery, provided they don't threaten 'operational efficiency'.)

Peter Smyth, defending counsel, asked Duncan if he was aware in the beginning that Susan was in love with him. He replied that he was.

'And did you love her?' Smyth asked.

'I loved her', Duncan replied, 'in what could be termed a friendship way or as a friend.'

'When you were having intercourse with Susan Christie did you tell her that you loved her?'

'No. Not as far as I can recall. I may well have done.'

Then Duncan qualified this. His words caused Susan to sob openly.

'I would tell her, "I love you, but not in the same way I love Penny." I stated at all times and I qualified it at all times that there was no future for us. I made it quite clear that I was not going to leave my wife and that I did not love her in the same way as I loved my wife.'

When Duncan left the witness box there must have been few people in the courtroom who thought he'd behaved as an officer and a gentleman.

It was Susan Christie's turn to offer her testimony. Peter Smyth asked her to give a brief account of her life and background, which she did. Smyth then moved on to her affair with Duncan. Susan contradicted many of the statements her lover had made under oath.

'Captain McAllister', Smyth said, 'has told the court that he loved you as a friend, that he would make it clear to you that it was not the same sort of love as between a man and a woman. What do you say to that?'

'He never said that to me. He told me that he loved me. And I believed him.'

Smyth asked if Penny was aware of the affair.

'If Penny was, then she never showed it to me. She was not that sort of person.'

The pregnancy came under discussion. What had been Duncan's reaction to the news?

'He was alarmed at first and then became more worried about me, that I might run and tell my family. He didn't want me to go and tell my mum and dad that I was pregnant before we'd talked things through.'

'And what was his attitude?' Smyth asked.

'Duncan said that I could either have an abortion, and he would support me emotionally afterwards,' Susan answered tearfully. 'Or that I could keep the baby but if I did so I'd have to leave the diving club and never talk to him again. If I said he was the father he'd deny it. He also told me that he'd be shipping out immediately from Ulster and I'd never see him again.'

'Captain McAllister has said in evidence there were three options,' Smyth said.

'No, he's lying. He told me that if I said he was the father he'd deny it and he'd never leave Penny for me.'

Duncan was winning no brownie points with the jury.

'Did you want the baby?'

'Yes. I wanted the baby.'

'And what was Captain McAllister's attitude?'

'He wanted me to have an abortion. He kept telling me that if I loved him I would have an abortion. He wanted to give me some telephone numbers that he found in the *Belfast Telegraph*, but I wouldn't take them.'

Smyth then moved on to the miscarriage. In between bouts of weeping, Susan told the court of Duncan's uncaring attitude to her and the baby she supposedly had lost. Supposedly, because we have only Susan Christie's word that she was ever pregnant at all; she admitted to lying to Duncan about seeing a doctor. She conceded that her miscarriage might have been a heavy period yet was adamant that a home pregnancy test had shown positive.

Again Duncan's coldness was revealed to the court. According to Susan he told her she was being 'over-emotional'.

'He kept telling me, "You're going for a commission and you're going to be an officer. You do not show your feelings."'

Peter Smyth led Susan up to the final weeks, when she'd been preparing to leave for Beaconsfield. The court heard that Duncan and she had continued to have sex together, though she claimed to have been unhappy and moody most of the time. Duncan, she said, told her he loved her only when asked. He refused to discuss their future.

It was at this point that Susan attempted to blacken the name of the innocent young woman she'd murdered so viciously. She claimed that Penny had tried to murder *her* during a scuba-dive. She'd got into difficulties; and Penny took so long in getting to her that it crossed Susan's mind 'that she was trying to kill me'.

'And is there any substance whatsoever in that?' Smyth asked.

'No. No, I mean she was not. I just felt at the time that she was trying to kill me.'

Eventually Susan was asked to testify about the killing of Penny McAllister. She told Smyth that the walk in the forest had been her idea.

'What do you say', he asked, 'about the allegation that you killed Mrs Penny McAllister in that forest on that afternoon?'

'I accept it.'

'Do you remember anything about it?'

'I remember parts of it.'

'Do you remember having a knife?'

'No.'

And so it went on, as Susan Christie claimed to remember not a thing about an attack, despite the many statements she'd given to the police in the days following the murder. Once again she broke into tears.

'I remember running through the forest,' she blubbered. 'My leg was sore. When I left that forest I honestly believed we'd been attacked, and I did not believe it was me.'

She continued to deny having any memory of the attack. She remembered, she maintained, nothing about her stabbing Penny so viciously that the victim's head was almost severed.

The jurors did not believe her. Susan had planned the murder weeks – perhaps even months – in advance. Why then, when the time came, did her mind and memory let her down? After careful deliberation they returned a verdict of guilty.

Lord Justice Kelly then sentenced her to five years in prison. He was showing a high degree of leniency towards somebody whom the province of Ulster regarded as a cunning and brutal killer. In fact he had accepted that, 'monstrous' though the slaying was, it remained an 'irrational act'. Kelly was prepared to accept that the circumstances leading up to the murder had deranged Susan Christie's mind to some extent.

Five months later, however, three appeal judges decided that Susan had indeed been in her right mind.

'Christie', the most senior judge said, 'had a very considerable degree of residual responsibility for the killing which made a sentence of five years unduly lenient.'

So they added four more.

Susan Christie was never to show remorse for the murder of the innocent young woman whose only 'crime' was to be married to Duncan McAllister. While awaiting trial in Maghaberry remand centre in Lisburn, she never once expressed regret – or sympathy with Penny's husband and family.

Nicholas Davies, who wrote a full account of the case,

tells how she sent a letter to four of her soldier friends at the UDR headquarters where she'd been stationed. It was a few weeks after her arrest. The letter is peppered with coarse, barrack-room humour and shows that Susan was revelling in the celebrity status she'd achieved. She ended the letter with, 'Take care and watch your backs. Love, Sue.'

Davies suggests that those words, 'watch your backs', were no accident.

> She had never used that phrase in everyday chat or when saying 'goodbye' to anyone. Everyone who knew her, and has read that letter, believes that she wrote that last phrase deliberately, as a joke. The phrase, however, revealed Susan Christie's attitude to the murder of Penny McAllister, her total lack of sympathy, remorse or feeling for the person whose life she took in such a cold-blooded manner. As a joke it was nothing but obscene.

She was released from prison in October 1995, having served no more than four and a half years for the callous and vicious murder of a young woman. She was given a new identity, and her present whereabouts are unknown to all but a few.